Technology and Critical Literacy in Early Childhood

What a thrill to find a smart and accessible text written for teachers, teacher educators, and teacher education students that not only shows how technology integrates in early childhood literacy curriculum, but does so in a way that recognizes children as active, productive, and critical literacy users. Unique in providing theorization and examples embedded within critical literacy and social justice aims and approaches, this is the kind of resource that teachers and teacher education students need as support and encouragement to use technology with young children and to expand their notions of literacy.

—*Karen Wohlwend, Indiana University*

What do new technologies and new forms of communication mean for young children growing up in the twenty-first century? How are they shaping the mindsets, identities, and practices that impact their lives at home and at school? This book explores the intersection of technology and critical literacy, specifically addressing what ICTs afford critical literacy work with young children between ages three to eight. Inviting readers to enter classrooms where both technology and critical literacies are woven into childhood curricula and teaching, it brings together literacy, social studies, and science in critical and integrated ways. Real-world stories show the sights and sounds of children engaged with technology in the classroom and beyond.

Concise but comprehensive, the text provides strategies, theoretical frameworks, demonstrations of practice, and resources for teachers. Pedagogical features in each chapter engage readers in making connections to their own teaching situations. NCATE standards for including technology as an essential part of teacher education programs are addressed. While acknowledging how individual children employ ICT, the focus is on how new technologies can be positioned in early childhood learning communities as tools for engaging in more meaningful, authentic, and interesting learning.

Vivian Maria Vasquez is Professor in the School of Education, Teaching and Health at American University, USA.

Carol Branigan Felderman is Adjunct Professor and Student Teacher Supervisor in the School of Education, Teaching and Health at American University, USA.

Technology and Critical Literacy in Early Childhood

Vivian Maria Vasquez and
Carol Branigan Felderman

Routledge
Taylor & Francis Group

NEW YORK AND LONDON

First published 2013
by Routledge
711 Third Avenue, New York, NY 10017

Simultaneously published in the UK
by Routledge
2 Park Square, Milton Park, Abingdon, Oxon OX14 4RN

Routledge is an imprint of the Taylor & Francis Group, an informa business

© 2013 Taylor & Francis

The right of Vivian Maria Vasquez and Carol Branigan Felderman to
be identified as authors of this work has been asserted by them in
accordance with sections 77 and 78 of the Copyright, Designs and
Patents Act 1988.

Library of Congress Cataloging in Publication Data
Vasquez, Vivian Maria.
Technology and critical literacy in early childhood / Vivian Maria Vasquez,
Carol Branigan Felderman.
     p. cm.
   Includes bibliographical references and index.
   1. Language arts (Early childhood) 2. Education – Effect of
technological innovations on. 3. Educational technology. 4. Critical
pedagogy. I. Felderman, Carol Branigan. II. Title.
   LB1139.5.L35V38 2012
   372.6–dc23   2012008984

ISBN: 978-0-415-53950-0 (hbk)
ISBN: 978-0-415-53951-7 (pbk)
ISBN: 978-0-203-10818-5 (ebk)

Typeset in Bembo
by HWA Text and Data Management, London

SUSTAINABLE
FORESTRY
INITIATIVE

Certified Sourcing
www.sfiprogram.org
SFI-00555
The SFI label applies to the text stock.

Printed and bound in the United States of America by
Walsworth Publishing Company, Marceline, MO.

To my boys, TJ and Andy, for always keeping us heading for the second star to the right, and straight on 'till morning.
VMV

To Jim, Liam, and Lily.
CBF

Contents

Preface

This book focuses on what new technologies afford critical literacy work with young children between ages three to eight.

Children today are born and inducted into a world in which new technologies and new forms of communication are widespread. Therefore, they participate in the world with new mindsets, identities, and practices, which impact their lives at home and at school. This book sheds light on what this means for young children, between the ages of three and eight, growing up in the twenty-first century. Throughout, we explore the "technoliteracies" (Marsh, 2002, p.1) with which they engage from a critical literacy perspective. Marsh argues that the multi-modal textual competencies and semiotic choices of children referred to by Luke (2007) as netizens are not given sufficient space within current curriculum frameworks to support their learning. This book offers demonstrations of the sorts of technoliteracies used and produced by young children and why this matters for literacy teaching and learning in the twenty-first century. Most impressive are the ways in which the teachers in the book are able to build critical curriculum that makes use of new digital communicative tools from the children's interests, passions, and desires.

The children that you will meet come from diverse settings including cooperative schools, public schools, and private schools. The teachers you will meet include pre-service, in-service, and teacher leaders. We deliberately chose to represent a diverse set of classrooms and teachers to make the point that what we are talking about in this book is the kind of critical and technologically informed work for which all children should have access and that all teachers ought to try regardless of their years of experience.

In many education programs, literacy courses claim to be imbued with technology. Focused on technology specifically with three- to eight-year old children in different school settings including a learning coop, public school, and private school settings, this book features technology as an integral component of the literacy and early childhood curriculum through telling real-world stories describing the sights and sounds of children engaged with technology in the classroom and beyond. It is interdisciplinary, emphasizing what technology affords the work done in integrating language arts, science, and social studies. The classroom teachers whose stories we tell in this book are at different points in their careers from a pre-service teacher to a literacy leader.

Technology and Critical Literacy in Early Childhood is designed for educators interested in early childhood education and literacy programs—both at the pre-service and the in-service levels. The audience includes students and instructors in early childhood and literacy teacher education programs leading to initial and advanced certification. It is specifically intended for use in early literacy education courses and in integrated curriculum courses in such programs. Though the text as a whole might directly appeal to faculty and students in the field of early childhood education (both at the undergraduate and graduate levels), its practical examples grounded in research, theoretical sophistication, and clear language will also appeal to others, including early childhood practitioners who are not taking university courses and administrators, and presenters and attendees of professional development seminars sponsored by school districts.

Mapping out the Terrain of this Book

After the introductory chapter, in Chapter 2 we spend time in a publicly funded pre-K classroom in Washington DC and a first grade classroom in a public school in North Carolina to explore what happens when children have opportunities to play and work with technology. In particular, this chapter focuses on the use of VoiceThread, a digital communication tool whereby viewers or listeners are able to leave comments and commentary on the slides. Kristen, in the pre-K classroom, is a pre-service teacher who is currently working on her teaching credentials. Katie, the researcher in the first grade classroom, is a seasoned former elementary school teacher and literacy coach.

In Chapter 3, our focus is on the use of technology for doing social action work. In this chapter, we enter three classrooms: two pre-K classrooms, a Catholic school in Ontario, Canada, and a public school in Georgia, and a first grade classroom in a School for Arts and Sciences in Virginia. In these classrooms, the classroom teachers created spaces for taking up issues of importance to the children based on their inquiry questions and interests and used these to create a critical curriculum.

Chapters 4 and 5 look at the use of podcasting in a second grade classroom in a School for the Arts and Sciences in Virginia. The classroom teacher was Carol, co-author of this book and a veteran teacher. Chapter 4 focuses on language identity and Chapter 5 on the children's deconstruction of a public text.

In Chapter 6, we turn our attention to the critical analysis of a YouTube video advertising the Topsy Turvey Tomato Planter. Our focus is a cooperative school setting in the Washington DC area where five- and six-year-olds made problematic the gendered text and questioned the validity of the claims made by the Topsy Turvey manufacturers regarding being able to grow bigger and better tomatoes using their techniques and equipment. The chapter will provide a narrative account of the various critical learning opportunities that resulted from the analysis of the video and experimenting with growing tomatoes.

In Chapter 7, we enter another second grade classroom, this one in a private school in Washington DC. Laura, the classroom teacher, has taught for almost ten years and has been attempting to create spaces for critical literacies for the last two years. In this chapter, she takes us on her students' journey as photographers who used their photos as a way of exploring notions of positioning and perspective. Our intent in including a chapter on photography is based on a hope that many of you will have access to a camera and that some of what Laura tried in her classroom may provide a space for you to begin to explore the use of technology in your setting.

In Chapter 8, the final chapter, we revisit what we have learned from young children's engagements with technology. To do this work, we turn to Gee's principles of learning (2003) and Luke and Freebody's Four Resources Model (1999) as a way to talk about the need for teachers to learn from their students as a step toward negotiating new curricular spaces for working with technology in early childhood settings

Pedagogical Features

To help you imagine possibilities for working at the intersection of critical literacy and new technology, each chapter includes Reflection Points, pedagogical invitations (labeled "Try This") and Resource Boxes. We invite you to use these to imagine possibilities for doing some of the work shared in this book with your own students. We hope the stories we share here provide for you a sense of pleasure and delight so that you may create new spaces in which to travel beyond what you read.

Acknowledgments

Vivian Maria Vasquez

Writing this book was a social networking experience as I connected with colleagues, asked questions, shared my thoughts, and asked for help in finding resources using Facebook, Twitter, IM, and e-mail. As we neared submission of the manuscript, I couldn't help but think about when my interest in technology, using a computer in particular, started. Four people came to mind, so I'll thank them first because they were instrumental in my journey into the world of information communication technology. Andy Bilodeau taught me to play with the tools and imagine what was possible even during the days of my Radio Shack Tandy Laptop, when its slowness made me want to give it away or throw it away. Judith Newman created a space for me to find things to do with those tools. With her, I began to trust myself as a writer. Jackie Marsh demonstrated the power and potential of using technology with young children. The fourth person is the child at the center of my life—my son TJ. I am deeply moved as I watch him fearlessly take on tech challenge after tech challenge with great joy, passion, and desire. Watching him fuels my interest to continue to explore at the intersection of technology and early childhood from a critical literacy perspective. He reminds me every day how important this work is and how much more I have to learn.

Carol Felderman, my friend and colleague, you have been such a comfort to work with! I look forward to many more projects with you in the future. Barbara Comber, Hilary Janks, Jerry Harste, Alan Luke, Andy Manning, and Dorothy Menosky, you are with me always as I do what I do. Thank you for your unwavering support and encouragement through the years.

Naomi Silverman, there are no words. You hold the title of publisher, but that really does not describe the you that I respect, admire, and appreciate. You and Sonia Nieto have opened up spaces for me that have enriched my life. Thank you now and always.

Of course, thanks go out to my family: Lily, Reggie Sr., Nanay and Jim, Vickie Reggie Jr., Victor, Jen, Tita Tit, and our beloved Tita Glor for your excitement at all that I do even when some of it makes no sense.

Thank you to Katie Stover, Laura Herring, and Kristen Luppino for contributing powerful stories to this book and to Kevan Miller for letting me play in her classroom during our Critical Literacy Study Group days. Thanks to Brian Kissel for introducing me to Katie; Mariana Souto Manning for planting the seed for this book and for working with us during the proposal phase; and Karen Wohlwend and Katherine Bomer for their very thoughtful comments and ongoing support.

Finally thank you to all the children and their teachers whose stories we told in this book and those children in my life. You lead the way for my learning each and every day.

Carol Branigan Felderman

With much love, admiration, and honor, I sincerely thank you, Vivian Vasquez. Not only for inviting me to work with you on this book but for almost 10 years of support and guidance in my developing understandings of critical literacy (CL) in my early childhood/elementary classrooms and now in my university classes. I am so fortunate to have a mentor/teacher such as you but, more than that, to have such an incredible friend.

To Naomi Silverman, who guided this project, thank you for such an enthusiastic and inviting first try in the book publishing process. I also thank Bill Glenn and Jerry Harste for their sincere belief in my writing and research. Bill, I cannot thank you enough for supporting me so thoroughly and always at the ready to push my thoughts and challenge my philosophies in new, purposeful, and meaningful ways. Jerry, your thoughtful and constructive critiques on my writing via IM and e-mail I will always treasure. Your words and insights always extend beyond immediate writings and will forever provide advice that help me be a better writer, educator, and researcher.

To the Bailey's Critical Literacy Study Group, I thank you for an incredible journey through my days in the classroom at Bailey's, which brought about my research. Former principals Jean Frey and Jay McClain, thank you for believing in my practices and giving me the space to create, learn, and teach with my students. Your beliefs and dedication to education and children are deeply inspiring. Last, to my dear friend and colleague Sarah Vander Zanden, thank you for being the amazing person that you are and for always listening, especially when I no longer made sense.

A heartfelt thanks to my dad for always encouraging me and supporting my endeavors and to my mom for "saving a place" for my writing on the bookshelf. Mostly, to little Liam and Lily, who came into my life at different stages of this work, providing me with deeper insight and courage than I ever thought I had. Finally, to Jim, who stayed with me from the beginning of my work in education, including my first year in the classroom: You are a brave and very patient man. I love you.

Special Acknowledgments

Special thanks to the following people who shared their stories with us for inclusion in this book:

Laura Herring
Kristen Luppino
Mariana Souto-Manning
Katie Stover.

The authors are grateful to the following for permissions to reproduce images in this book:

Figure 1.1: Taylor Jose Vasquez Bilodeau
Figures 2.1–2.12 ©VoiceThread, 2011, http://www.voicethread.com, reproduced with permission
Figure 5.1; © ClustrMaps Ltd, 2011, www.clustrmaps.com, reproduced with permission
Figures 6.2, 6.6, and 7.4 © Tagxedo, 2011, http://www.tagxedo.com, reproduced with permission
Figures 7.1–7.4: Laura Herring.

Chapter 1

Setting a Context for Exploring Critical Literacies Using Technology

Figure 1.1 TJ's Family with iPods

The opening image (Figure 1.1) was drawn by Vivian's son TJ when he was five years old after he and his classmates were asked by his preschool teacher to make a picture of his family. While describing his drawing, he explained that each person in his family has an iPod Touch in their hand. Upon closer inspection, it becomes obvious each person has a different combination of colored dots on their iPods. When asked what the different colors represent, he explained that each person in his family has his or her own interests and, therefore, would have a different set of applications, which he referred to as "apps," on their iPods. For instance, he suggested that he would have games such as Rolando and Angry Birds on his iPod whereas his mother or father might have a grocery list application on theirs.

Four-year-old Hannah was in the car with her father. Upon noticing they were in an unfamiliar neighborhood, she suggested, "...use the GPS, Daddy."

Three-year-old Thomas had not been interested in giving up his pacifier until his parents suggested he could trade it for something he wanted. Without hesitation, he agreed. Luckily, his parents had an old laptop that they could trade with him. Now, he no longer has a pacifier in his mouth; instead, he sits at his table in front of his very own laptop.

Children such as TJ, Hannah, and Thomas are born and inducted into a world in which new technologies and new forms of communication are widespread. Janks and Vasquez (2011) note that today books can be immediately downloaded, music and images can be mixed and re-mixed and immediately retrieved using quick response codes. As such, there are new spaces in which children can produce and reproduce identities and enter global online communities (Janks and Vasquez, 2011). It should not be a surprise, then, that these new communicative tools have found their way into children's play: a site for the appropriation of cultural tools (Wohlwend, 2009). For instance, TJ "played" iPod using toys at his disposal before he ever had an actual iPod in his hand.

Changes in the communicative terrain have made it very difficult to "imagine what the landscape will look like by the time the generation currently in school will graduate" (Janks and Vasquez, 2011). This is especially true given the speed with which new communication technologies are being developed. Imagine, it was not too long ago when the most technology young children could get was sitting in front of the television watching *Sesame Street*. Today, the only certainty we can count on is that we cannot be certain as to what the future will demand of our young people. The best we can do is imagine possibilities. We hope that this book helps you to do just that—imagine ways of creating space to capitalize on what technology can afford the work that we do.

Differential Access to the New "Black Gold"

Nevertheless "where in some homes very young children are able to manipulate and create texts for touch screen smart phones, participate in massively multi-player online games such as, the once popular, Lego Universe, and play interactive games on computers, others remain without food, shelter, running water, and electricity" (Janks & Vasquez, 2011). Subsequently, Janks and Comber (2006) state that mobility, as in the ability to navigate space and time as a result of technological advances, is a class marker. More recently Janks and Vasquez (2011) have noted that connectivity is also a class marker and that social differences produce differential access to the world so that the world is more accessible to some than to others. This is what Wu (2010) refers to when he talks about bandwidth as the new black gold that produces new and diverse forms of inclusion and exclusion. On the one hand, we need to find ways to make the technology accessible to more children. On the other hand, we need to find ways to accept the challenge(s) of the new technological world in which we live to best support children such as TJ, Hannah, and Thomas, who participate in the world with new mindsets, identities, and practices that impact their lives at home, at school, and beyond. This book sheds light on what this means for young children, between the ages of three and eight, growing up in the twenty-first century.

Marsh (2002) argues that the multi-modal textual competencies and semiotic choices of children referred to by Luke (1999) as *netizens* are not given sufficient space within current curriculum frameworks to support their learning. In response, the chapters that follow create space for thinking about how to create such spaces by exploring the technoliteracies (Marsh, 2002) with which children engage from a critical literacy perspective. Throughout, we offer demonstrations of these technologically based literacies as they are used and produced by young children and why this matters for literacy teaching and learning in the twenty-first century. What differentiates this book from many others is that the teachers whose classrooms we enter frame the work they do using new technologies from a critical literacy perspective. This is not a widely used intersection for working with young children. Further, the work presented here primarily focuses on curriculum that stems from the inquiry questions and passions of the children: building on their diverse lived experiences and their funds of knowledge (Moll, Amanti, Neff, & Gonzalez, 1992). Throughout, we show and tell about what happens when teachers capitalize on opportunities for using technology and critical literacy based on matters of importance to children or based on a desire to make accessible to them new ways of communicating their ideas.

New Technologies as Tools for Engaging in Critical Literacy Work

Critical literacy has been a topic of contestation for some time. This, in part, is due to the belief that it should look, feel, and sound different and accomplish different sorts of life work depending on the context in which it is being used, as a theoretical and pedagogical framework for teaching and learning (Luke, 2007; Vasquez, 2001, 2004; Comber & Simpson, 2001). Vivian (Vasquez, 1994) has referred to this framing as a way of being, where she has argued that critical literacy should not be an add-on but a frame through which to participate in the world. As such, there is no such thing as a critical literacy text. The world as text, however, can be read from a critical literacy perspective. What this means is that the issues and topics of interest that capture learners' interests as they participate in the world around them can and should be used as text to build a curriculum that has significance in their lives and that are developmentally sensible. Following are key tenets that comprise a critical literacy perspective. These tenets are informed by work done by Luke and Freebody (1999) and their Four Resources Model; Janks's (2010) Interrelated Model for Critical Literacy; Comber's work on critical literacy in the early years (2001); and Marsh's work on new technologies (2005).

- Critical literacy involves having a critical perspective or stance (Vasquez, 2004; 1994)
  Critical literacy should, therefore, be seen as a perspective from which to engage in the day-to-day living in a classroom rather than as a unit of study that lasts for a predetermined amount of time.
- Students' cultural knowledge and multi-modal literacy practices should be utilized (Comber, 2001; Vasquez, 1998)
  What this means is that students' funds of knowledge and diverse ways of practicing literacy are privileged in the curriculum.
- The world is a socially constructed text that can be read (Frank, 2008)
  This tenet draws on Freire and Macedo's (1987) notion that when we read the word, we simultaneously read the world.
- Texts are never neutral (Freebody and Luke, 1990)
  What this means is all texts are socially constructed. That is, texts are created by someone from a particular standpoint, position, point of view, or stance. As such, there is nothing natural or normal about any text, whether this be a book or a text from everyday life such as an advertisement flyer or cereal box.
- Texts work to create particular subject positions that make it easier or harder for us to say and do certain things; therefore, we need to interrogate the perspective(s) presented through texts (Meacham, 2003).
  This means that texts are not only socially constructed; they are also socially constructive offering particular ways of being, doing, talking, and thinking that shift from context to context.
- We read from (a) particular subject position(s), and so our readings of texts are never neutral, and we need to interrogate the position(s) from which we read (speak, act, do…)
  Just as no text is neutral, natural, or normal, our reading of a text is never neutral, natural, or normal, either. Our readings of text are rooted in our discursive practices and the cultural models through which we live our lives.
- What we claim to be true or real is always mediated through discourse (Gee, 1999).
  We can never speak outside of discourse. As we engage with text or other people, we bring with us ways of being, doing, and thinking that help shape what we say and do.
- Critical literacy involves understanding the sociopolitical systems in which we live.
  This refers to the fact that how we choose to teach, the decisions that we make, are political decisions (Janks, 2010). Understanding this is a first step in developing political awareness that helps us to better unpack why things are the way they are and how things could be different.
- Critical literacy practices can contribute to change (Freire & Macedo, 1987; Freebody & Luke, 1990; Vasquez, 2004).

This builds on the position that all texts are socially constructed. As texts are socially constructed, it follows that texts can be deconstructed and reconstructed for the purpose of changing problematic ways of being or doing.

- Text design and production can provide opportunities for critique and transformation (Larson and Marsh, 2005; Vasquez, 2005; Janks, 1993).

Before we are able to redesign a text, we must first figure out what about that text is so problematic that we need for it to be reconstructed. This process of figuring out what is problematic then creates a space for critique and transformation.

The last tenet, which states that text design and production can provide opportunities for critique and transformation, is really where new technologies and social media could have a strong role. Text design and production refer to the creation or construction of texts and the decisions that are part of that process. This includes the notion that it is not sufficient to simply create texts for the sake of practicing a skill. If children are to create texts, they ought to be able to let those texts do the work intended. For instance, if children are writing surveys or creating petitions, they ought to be done with real-life intent for the purpose of dealing with a real issue. If children write petitions, they ought to be able to send them to whomever they were intended for. Helping children understand real-life functions of text is an important component of growing as a critically literate individual (Vasquez, 2005 ; Luke and Freebody, 1999).

Over the years, there have been growing accounts of critical literacy work in classrooms (Vasquez, 1994, 1999, 2001, 2005; Vasquez and Egawa, 2003; O'Brien, 2001; Comber, 2001; Morgan, 1997). However, as mentioned earlier, there are very limited accounts in the literature on the ways new technologies intersect with critical literacies. This book is our attempt to contribute to filling that gap.

The two of us have a long history of creating spaces for critical literacies in our various settings. Vivian began her exploration while she was a preschool and elementary school teacher in the 1980s, whereas Carol began her exploration of critical literacy as part of a teacher study group facilitated by Vivian from 2001 to 2008. Vivian taught preschool (birth to four) and primary school-age children (four to eight) in Canada for fourteen years whereas Carol taught primary school-aged children in the United States for approximately ten years.

The two of us met in 2001 as participants in a study group of teachers creating spaces for critical literacies in a school just outside of Washington, DC. We came together through a common interest to find ways to best support young children and early childhood educators to create space for critical literacy in their setting.

Extending Children's Repertoire of Literacy and Communications Practices

Comber, Nixon, and Reid (2007) note that in the teaching of literacy, our role as teachers includes extending the repertoires of literacy and communications practices available to our students. They talk about a pedagogy of responsibility (2007), which they state involves "…classroom practice that is informed and structured by teachers' commitment to engaging with questions of diversity and democracy…" (p. 14) with their students. Place-based pedagogies, they say, foreground the local and the known and are opportunities for teachers "to structure learning and communication experiences around the things that are most meaningful to their students: their own places, people and popular cultures, and concerns" (p. 14). How might technology, such as sending a message or text using a cell phone, creating a video, and participating in online spaces such as electronic art galleries for children, provide new, interesting, and different ways for children to communicate their ideas, questions, and understanding about the world around them?

Lankshear and Knobel (2007) believe that alongside new technical stuff comes new ethos. New technical stuff refers to living in a digital culture, or digitality, and what that affords: connectivity, social networking, and instant information. The new ethos stuff refers to a shift of mindset, or way of thinking about technology use, as a result of the new technical stuff. What new things can we do, in terms of literacy teaching and learning, with the use of this new technology? What can we do differently in our teaching as a result of this new technology? How can we make meaning differently as a result of new technology? What can new technologies and social media afford our work with critical literacy. This question rings especially true in the area of text design (creating texts), redesign (taking existing texts, critiquing their construction, and then creating new texts), and production (producing or constructing texts). As noted earlier, we refer to texts as broadly construed and not limited (for instance, to print-based or image-based text).

New Technologies ≠ Critical Literacy

We want to be clear that the use of new technologies and social media does not constitute engagement with critical literacies. Just because one is using new technology in the classroom, it does not mean they are simultaneously engaging in critical literacies. Rather, these new technologies and social media can be used as tools to carry out our critical literacy work. They help us to think and make meaning differently. Such tools can be used to think differently about texts, in the production of texts, and also in the distribution of texts both locally and globally. Throughout this book, we share stories, insights, and resources on how, in different settings with young children, we have worked to examine, produce, and distribute texts using new technological tools and doing so from a critical literacy perspective.

The children whom you will meet come from diverse settings including cooperative schools, public schools, and private schools. To respect their privacy, we have used pseudonyms throughout.

The teachers you will meet include pre-service, in-service, and teacher leaders. We deliberately chose to represent a diverse set of classrooms and teachers to make the point that what we are talking about in this book is the kind of critical and technologically informed work to which all children should have access and all teachers ought to try regardless of their years of experience.

Resource Box 1.1

 Texts that Focus on Critical Literacy and Technology

Comber, B., & Kamler B. (2005). (Eds). *Turn-around Pedagogies*. NSW: Newtown.

Comber, B. & Simpson, A. (2001). *Negotiating Critical Literacies in Classrooms*. New York, NY: Routledge.

Gee, J. P., & Hayes, E. R. (2011). *Language and Learning in the Digital Age*. New York, NY : Routledge

Janks, H. (2010). *Literacy and Power*. New York, NY: Routledge.

Larson, J. & Marsh, J. (2005). *Making Literacy Real*. Thousand Oaks, CA: Sage.

Marsh, J. (2002). Popular culture, computer games and the primary curriculum. In M. Monteith (Ed.), *Teaching Primary Literacy through ICT* (pp. 127–143). Buckinghamshire: Open University Press.

Marsh, J. (2005). (Ed). *Popular Culture, New Media and Digital Literacy in Early Childhood*. New York, NY: Routledge Press.

Marsh, J., et al. (2005). *Digital Beginnings: Young People's Use of Popular Culture, Media and New Technologies*. Sheffield,UK: University of Sheffield Research Center.

Vasquez, V. (2004). *Negotiating Critical Literacies with Young Children*. New York, NY: Routledge.

Vasquez, V. (2010). *Getting Beyond "I Like the Book": Creating Space for Critical Literacy in K–6 Classrooms* (2nd ed.). Newark, DE: International Reading Association.

Wohlwend, K. (2011). *Playing Their Way into Literacies*. New York, NY: Teachers College Press.

Chapter 2

Teaching and Learning with VoiceThread

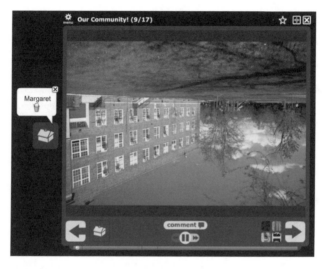

Figure 2.1 Margaret's Favorite Picture

The opening image is a slide that Kristin Lupino and her four-year-old students created using VoiceThread. They felt it reminded them of a building they saw during a community walk. The intent of the walk was to notice things they saw along the way. After the walk, the children talked about things they saw for which Kristen created a VoiceThread slide show. Sometime later, the children were asked to choose their favorite from the selection of images that Kristen had put together. The photo in Figure 2.1 was chosen by Margaret even though one of the children had played with the image and turned it upside down.

In this chapter, we enter two early childhood classrooms to explore what VoiceThread afforded teaching and learning in those classrooms and what children did as they played and worked with this digital communication tool. In the first classroom, we spend time with a former graduate student of ours,

Kristin Lupino, who was teaching fifteen four-year-old preschool children. The school is a Title 1 Public School in Washington, DC, where 70 percent of the children receive free or reduced lunch. In her class, there were children who spoke different languages: English, Spanish, Mandarin, Arabic, and French. Kristin was at the school for a weekly practicum experience, which was part of her teacher certification. She spent one day a week observing and interacting with children. She also was given the opportunity to teach children the use of technology. She had heard of VoiceThread being enjoyed by the fourth graders and thought perhaps the younger children might enjoy it also. At the time that she worked in this classroom, Kristen had just started exploring opportunities for taking up critical literacy and using technology in early childhood classrooms.

Katie Stover, a doctoral candidate at the University of North Carolina at Charlotte and a former elementary teacher and literacy coach, brought the second classroom we will talk about to our attention. Carol met Katie through a mutual friend and colleague. The classroom was Katie's research site for a qualitative case study with one first grade class at a public charter school located in a suburban area outside of Charlotte, NC. The purpose of her study was to explore what happened when young children engaged in collaborative and critical discussions of social issues such as racism, sexism, and bullying using children's literature as a springboard. VoiceThread was a tool used for sharing the work they were doing. Unlike Kristen, the teacher in the classroom in which Katie was doing her research was not new to critical literacy or the use of technology in schools.

What is VoiceThread?

According to the company Web site (2012) "[a] VoiceThread is a collaborative, multimedia slide show that holds images, documents, and videos and allows people to navigate slides and leave comments in five ways—using voice (with a mic or telephone), text, audio file, or video (via a webcam"; retrieved from http://voicethread.com/) What this means is that when you share a VoiceThread with friends, family, colleagues, or anyone else you would like, they are able to record comments in audio, video, or text format directly on the image itself. Figure 2.2 is a screen shot that shows a text comment posted on a slide.

At the time that this book was published, free accounts were available at VoiceThread. The free account allows you to do three minutes of phone commenting, three slide shows at a time with up to fifty slides each, and unlimited voice and text comments. You are also provided with limited webcam commenting capabilities, so you can do quite a bit with a Free VoiceThread account! To set up an account go to https://voicethread.com/ and click on the register or sign-in link on the top right-hand corner of the homepage.

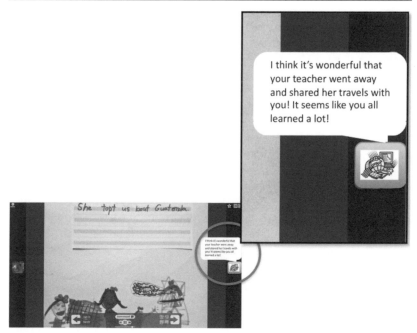

Figure 2.2 VoiceThread Comment

Kristin

> I was lucky to have a computer lab and a tech teacher who allowed 4-year-olds in the lab.

In spite of growing accounts of young children's use of technology (Marsh, 2005; Evans, 2005; Bers, 2008; Vasquez, 2010b), there continues to be resistance to its use in early childhood settings. Kristen's comment that she was lucky to have computer lab access, therefore, makes sense. And yet, as noted by Carrington (2005, p. 13), "…young people are immersed in textual landscapes that are no longer print dominated." She continues: "This has implications for the skills and knowledge they bring with them to literacy instruction and for the worlds of work and leisure in which they will live out their lives" (2005, p. 13).

In our conversations with early childhood teachers, a primary cause for resistance seems to be a worry that young children are not ready for computer use and, therefore, could cause damage to expensive equipment. Some early-years teachers also worry that working with technology is isolating and what children need are opportunities to grow and learn from one another and to engage in real-world conversations, meaning face-to-face exchanges. In this chapter, we disrupt these notions by showing and telling about how two groups of young children engaged in pleasurable and meaningful social experiences as they worked with technology in their classrooms.

Playing with VoiceThread

During a conference presentation in Fall 2011, Kristen shared her goals for working with VoiceThread.

> Kristen's goals for working with VoiceThread:
> - Identify familiarity with technology
> - Increase computer access and literacy
> - Learn how to type own name
> - Evaluate effectiveness of VoiceThread for use with four-year-olds.

She wanted to first find out the children's familiarity and facility with computers. She also wanted them to learn the parts of the computer and how to key in their names. She started by first talking to the children about what rules they should follow when using the computers in the lab. Following are the rules they came up with, for which Kristen created a wall chart.

Rules

- Be nice to the computer
- No food or drink
- Be quiet.

Kristen

> I was really impressed by the rules they came up with. We did this before we went and carried them with us. The student who came up with the "No food or drink" rule helped explain why the rule was important.

Kristen shared that almost half of the students in the class had access to computers at home. What is most interesting about the rules the children suggested is that each one is indicative of the historical body (Scollon & Scollon, 2004) of the student, that is, their life experiences and unconscious ways of thinking and being (Scollon & Scollon, 2004). The child who contributed the "No food or drink" rule, for instance, shared that the reason why there should be no food or drink by the computers is because "The computer will get messed up." He continued, "My mommy spilled coffee on hers. She can't use it now." Young children very quickly learn about practices such as being quiet, being nice, and being careful both in and out of school. These practices quickly become habituated (Bourdieu, 1977), naturalized, or normalized ways of being. These same practices are often exaggerated in spaces where technology use is taking place. In other settings, for instance, Vivian has observed adults telling children to keep their hands on their laps while instructions are being given regarding computer use. This was

Figure 2.3 Kahlil's Image

part of the being careful rule and getting children "ready" for doing work on the computer.

Kristen wanted the children to be mindful of how they treated the computers, but mostly she wanted them to experience the sorts of learning that could be produced through the use of technology. For instance, she noticed that the children were finding it difficult to locate certain keys, so to help them out she did things such as putting a green dot on the correct button or a yellow star on another button. What she discovered is that this simple solution made it that much easier for the children to navigate the keyboard. A disadvantage of having little hands is managing commands that required holding down more than one key at a time.

Prior to creating their own VoiceThread, Kristen created one using images of vegetables that went into a soup that the children had made with their classroom teacher. She then let them freely explore and play to experience the software. After this, during her next visit with the children, she took them on a community walk, after which time they created "Our Community," a VoiceThread that was made up of images of things they saw during their walk. While viewing the various images that made up their community walk slide show, Kristen asked the children to choose their favorite slide and tag it by posting their name in a comment box. Figure 2.3 is the image Kahlil chose. His name was keyed in as a comment on the left-hand side of the image.

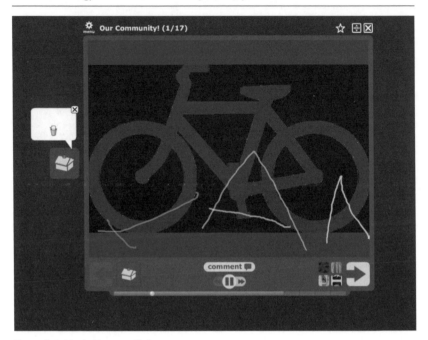

Figure 2.4 Xan's Favorite Slide

So far so good. The children seemed to be doing what Kristen had expected. She soon realized that the written lesson plan, what Manning (1993) refers to as the envisaged curriculum, the paper curriculum that is handed to teachers through state mandates or curriculum guides, is not always the curriculum that the children follow. Before she knew it, the "real curriculum" (Manning, 1993, p. 2) began to unfold. According to Manning, the real curriculum "…is what goes on in the mind of the student…the lived through experience…the sense they make of what is going on in [the] classroom" (1993, p. 2).

Some children took Kristen's instructions quite literally when she told them to put their name on the image. In Figure 2.4, for example, Xan actually took the drawing tool and wrote his name on top of the image. The bar at the bottom of the image with the small dot on it indicates that he took quite a bit of time to write his name. This was not something that he did quickly; he took a long time to draw his name on the image. On VoiceThread, every comment, whether it is written or vocalized, is recorded, which makes it possible to know how long it took for someone to leave their comment. The farther the dot has slid toward the right side of the bar, the longer the recording.

Other children chose to doodle, draw, and scribble over the image rather than inserting their name. Yet others decided to play and explore possibilities doing things such as inverting images and putting marks down over those images. Valeria even went so far as to use different colors as she drew. At the

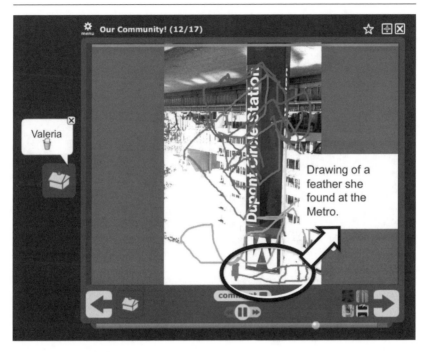

Figure 2.5 Valeria's Feather

bottom of the image, she also drew a feather that she had found at the base of the metro sign (see Figure 2.5). Taylor did multiple things on the image he chose. In Figure 2.6, he tagged the image with his name and traced the image of a bicycle using different colors. Other children discovered how to play with various controls such as brightening and dimming the page. Then there were occasions when copious amounts of repeated single letters were printed across a slide as the children were learning to manipulate the keys on the keyboard and control the mouse. This called for orienting their bodies, their fingers, hands, and arm in relation to the components of the computer. Underlying skills to be learned are sometimes invisible because the learning curve, especially with children who are born into a world of technology, is quite steep. They often develop multiple skills and competencies simultaneously as they engage in the complex dance steps that, in the case of the VoiceThread slide, led to positioning letters onto an image. The children had to work out not only how to control their hand on the mouse and the mouse itself so that they were able to position it just so on the image; they then had to figure out how hard or soft to press on the keys and so forth. Supporting all this new exploration was not always easy. Kristen noted, "As a student teacher, helping each of the 15 4-year-olds was particularly difficult, because I had little to no help from any other adult in the room." Regardless, she kept at it.

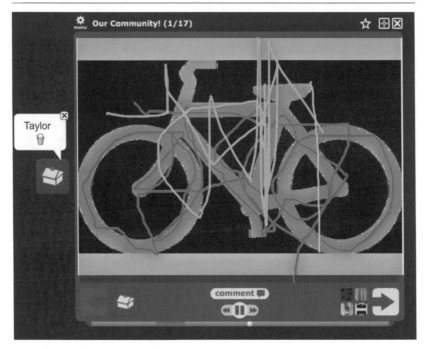

Figure 2.6 Taylor's Name Tag and Drawing

Kristen

> The students accomplished so much more on the site than I even knew was possible. It was interesting and unexpected.

Although she got to meet with them only five times, she was encouraged by her observations that by the children's fifth time playing on the computers, thirteen out of fifteen of them were able to confidently log on and go to VoiceThread. The most challenging aspect, she discovered, was for them to log on the school's password-protected computers. To do this, the children needed help in using a ctrl-alt-delete function to open the login command. What this means is that to log on, the children had to hold down three buttons at once; control, alt, and delete. This is often a step required of networked computers; computers that are connected together within one network or system.

Kristin also observed that by their fifth day on the computers, eight of fifteen students were able to key in their names even though some of these same children could not yet write their names on paper. This and the ways in which some children were able to use the VoiceThread tools to visually articulate what they found interesting during their walk (see Figure 2.5) showed that for the children Kristen worked with, the use of technology afforded a space for communicating and representing that was different than crayons on paper. While sharing the slide she was working on (see Figure 2.5), Valeria asked, "[Do you] see the feather I found at the metro?" Kristin's acknowledgment that she indeed could see the feather reaffirmed to Valeria that she had successfully communicated her observation.

Clearly, what we think we are teaching is not necessarily what they are learning. In Kristen's case, the children had learned so much more than what she had laid out as goals for them to accomplish during their time together.

Goal No.1 called for the children to become familiar with technology. Following is what they accomplished:

- Location of particular keys on the keyboard
- How to physically handle the mouse and the keys
- Locating particular programs for use
- How to work with the digital pen
- Computers and drinks are not a good combination.

Goal No. 2 was to increase computer access and literacy. Following is what they accomplished:

- Weekly visits to the computer lab took place while Kristin was doing her practicum.
- Most of the children were able to locate and log on to VoiceThread
- Drawing objects using the digital pen
- Using different colors in their drawing
- Purposeful and meaningful communication
- Creating for an audience
- Representing and communicating thinking and knowing
- Refer to Goals 1 and 3 for more.

Goal No. 3 was for the children to learn to learn to type their own name. Following is what they accomplished:

- Recognizing, naming, and finding letters on the keyboard
- Eight of fifteen of the children were able to key in their names.
- Writing their name using the digital pen
- Using different colors in their writing.

Even the complicated log-in process did not dissuade the children from carrying on. In spite of many failed attempts at trying to do various things on the computer, the children plugged away at it. Gee (2005) had the same experience while learning to play a video game:

As I confronted the game I was amazed. It was hard, long, and complex. I failed many times and had to engage in a virtual research project via the Internet to learn some of things I needed to know. All my Baby-Boomer ways of learning and thinking didn't work. I felt myself using learning muscles that hadn't had this much of a workout since my graduate school days in theoretical linguistics.

As I struggled, I thought: Lots of young people pay lots of money to engage in an activity that is hard, long, and complex. As an educator, I realized that this was just the problem our schools face: How do you get someone to learn something long, hard, and complex and yet enjoy it? (p. 34)

The four-year-olds Kristen worked with found their task pleasurable. Given the kinds of things they did as part of the "real curriculum," this is likely because they were doing what they had to do, to do what they wanted to do (i.e., draw an image on the slide to accompany the existing image, as in Valeria's feather). It seems they did what they did as they played with various possibilities presented by the VoiceThread software. In essence, they were simultaneously playing and working, and Kristin created a space for them to do just that.

REFLECTION POINT 2.1

- What are some ways you might use VoiceThread in your curriculum?
- What might you focus on? How will you decide?
- What different role(s) might you have children play?
- How would you deal with the logistics involved in using computers with young children?

Using VoiceThread for Social Action

The image in Figure 2.7 was created by one of the first graders from Katie Stover's research on critical literacy and writing. *We Can Help* is written in large colorful letters across almost the entire page. Underneath the words we find two groups of people representing the children from the class and, therefore, the agents out to help. Katie shared with us some background information pertaining to her research:

This study gives an inside look at how young writers reconstruct text and used their voices to advocate for social justice. After several weeks of collaborative and critical literacy discussions, students worked in collaborative writing groups to choose a topic of interest, write for an authentic purpose, and publish their writing for a wide audience using Voicethread.com.

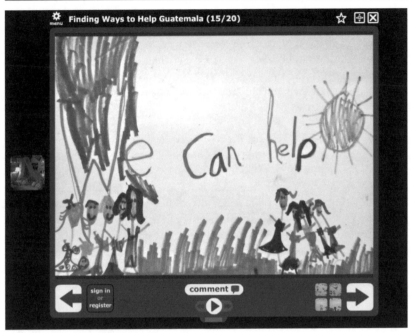

Figure 2.7   We Can Help

Try This 2.1

Playing with Perspectives, Stances, or Identities

One unique feature of VoiceThread is that while commenting, you can take on multiple identities, represented by different avatars on one account. This means you do not have to sign in using different accounts, unlike other social networking tools. A demonstration is available at http://voicethread.com/about/features/identities/# This element has the potential use of creating a space for children to put on offer different comments while trying on different perspectives, stances, or identities. This would be a wonderful way for children to be able to look at topics/issues from different orientations or points of view. They could play with those different ways of looking at the slide(s) to make a more informed decision about that topic/issue.

Those worried about who might leave comments for the children, because their work is posted in a public space, may find comfort in knowing the owner of a VoiceThread is able to pick which comments are shown using the moderation feature that is part of the software. VoiceThreads can also be inserted on other Web sites and receive comments on those sites or be exported and downloaded to a portable media device, such as an iPod, and burned to DVD.

"One Hand Cannot Clap"

> We have an expression in the native Dinka language that Manute Bol and I share: "One hand cannot clap." I have learned on my journey of trying to build schools, that it is too hard to do it alone. Collaboration across tribes, villages, religions, countries and organizations is key to our ability to make dreams come true (James Lubo Mijak, 2010).

Manute Bol was a very well-known NBA basketball star who passed way in 2010 leaving behind a dream to build schools in his native Sudan. Bol was reported to have contributed most of his earnings to help bring this dream to life. In particular, he wanted to help the "Lost Boys" of Sudan and other refugees. The name Lost Boys of Sudan or *Lost Boys*, according to a film by the same name, was given to a group of Southern Sudanese boys by United Nations aid workers who were monitoring their flight from war-torn Sudan. Many of these children who were orphaned or displaced walked for weeks and months seeking refuge in places such as Ethiopia, Uganda, and Kenya. Through the work of several agencies and organizations families in the United States adopted some of these boys. James Lubo Mijak, or Lubo, as he is better known, was one such boy. His adoptive family lives in North Carolina, and one of his adoptive family members was in the class observed by Katie. Now an adult, he recounts working his way through college and becoming a financial analyst in Charlotte, NC in 2011, where he can carry on the legacy left by Bol. In a news interview with Reinl (2011), Lubo said, "It has always been in my heart to go back and help [build schools]…We don't have enough educated people…"

Helping Lubo

One group of students from Katie's research used their writing to inform a broader audience about Lubo and his dream to build a school in his home village of Southern Sudan. Different from Kristin's work with the four-year-old children, the children in Katie's study used VoiceThread as a tool for taking specific social action. Like the children you will meet in Chapter 3, these children used technology to do work with social effects that contribute to changed conditions of living or being. Their text includes a series of ten slides. The first five slides introduce the topic and offer definitions for the term *Lost Boy* (See Figure 2.8 Defining "Lost Boy")

The next two slides describe Lubo, and the last three slides offer ways of helping him. One of these slides also describes what various donation amounts would pay for in terms of school supplies such as a literacy kit and art materials for one child ($35.00) or cement blocks for the structure itself, which costs $20 per block. In total, it would cost $200,000.00 to build a school that would accommodate 300 children.

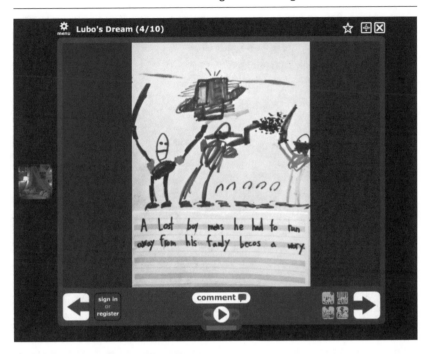

Figure 2.8 Defining "Lost Boy"

Helping a School in Guatemala

In their second VoiceThread, the children shift their focus toward finding ways to help a school in Guatemala. This text consisted of twenty slides. Unlike Helping Lubo, this series of slides begins with setting a context for why the children have decided on the topic: Their teacher had gone to Guatemala and told them about her visit and the school. They then make visible their privileges in life by naming some ways in which they are privileged. For instance, one slide talks about liking musical instruments, implying that they have access to such instruments, whereas another says they all have families (see Figure 2.9). For us, this is a wonderful demonstration of the ways in which children are able to unpack the position(s) from which they speak.

From here, they turn to the Guatemalan children and what they have been told by their teacher who visited Guatemala, and they identify some things the children might need in their school (see Figure 2.10).

Interesting to note is the inclusion of such items as jumps ropes and musical instruments alongside books and other such materials. More than often in the spirit of "helping" children in other countries, the first things on the list of things to gather are school supplies such as pens, pencils, and books. Here, the children could be drawing on their own experiences and their own needs and wants

Figure 2.9 Naming Privilege

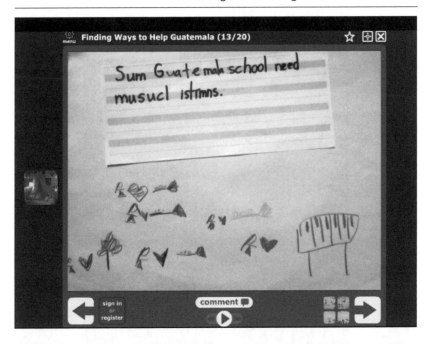

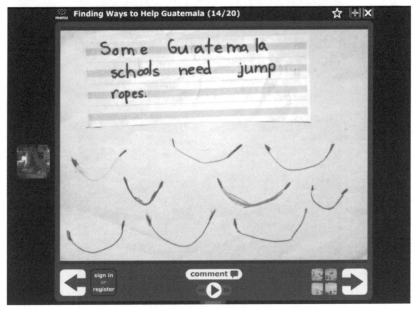

Figure 2.10 What the Guatemalan Children Need

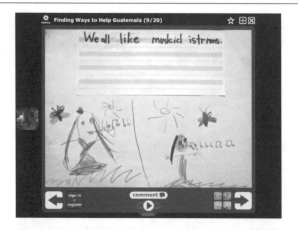

Figure 2.11 "BUT"

Figure 2.12   Raise Money

as a basis for imagining what Guatemalan children might need and want. The transition from their position of privilege to what the Guatemalan children need happens with a slide that simply says "BUT" (see Figure 2.11)

The final slides in the VoiceThread encourage viewers to either donate money or raise money (see Figure 2.12).

Katie

> The goal of my research was to provide an alternative approach to scripted instruction that can stifle children's abilities to interact with text in deeper, more meaningful ways. This approach to literacy instruction can help transition young children into knowledgeable, capable, and productive citizens who shape the world into a more just and equitable place.

Clearly, the work done by the children to raise funds for not only one but two causes is a good demonstration of what happens when children are given opportunities to be what Katie describes as "productive citizens who shape the world into a more just and equitable place." Through their VoiceThread slides, the children were able to persuade viewers to donate time, money, or resources to help Lubo's cause of building a school in South Sudan and to support a school in Guatemala.

We asked Katie what resulted from the children's efforts.

Katie

Over a two-week period of time, the students raised more than three hundred dollars and split the donations evenly between the two organizations (Raising South Sudan [to support Lubo] and Project LEAP [to support the Guatemalan children]). With approximately one hundred and fifty dollars for each non-profit organization, students' fund raising provided approximately 80 cement blocks for the structure of the school building in South Sudan and countless supplies, including books written in Spanish, games, and instructional materials for the school in Guatemala.

Re-negotiating Curricular Spaces

At the start of the chapter, Kristen showed us what happens when we as adults remain open to re-negotiating the curriculum. If she had made the children stick to exactly what she had originally intended for them to do, they would not have been able to develop some of the literacy skills and competencies that arose as a result of their play with the software.

Similarly, the students with whom Katie worked, through their slides, showed a commitment to their learning because what they were doing had importance in their lives. What was important to them was to be able to contribute to the changing conditions of living for others in other spaces and places in the world and that is exactly what they did.

In the next chapter, we visit three more early childhood settings where children and teachers engage in social action projects with real-world effects using various technological tools.

Chapter 3

Yes We Can!
Using Technology as a
Tool for Social Action

Stefanie:	Rainforest animals are in danger.
Curtis:	What?
Lee:	It's true. Look here (referring to a printout from the Internet describing rainforest animals being in danger of extinction).
Curtis:	That is NOT good.
Ali:	What should we do to help?
Lee:	Ya. Maybe we understand, but maybe they don't understand…

Prior to working as a college professor, Vivian taught preschool and elementary school for fourteen years. This opening vignette took place while she was teaching Pre-K. In Vivian's classroom for three- to five-year-olds, children were positioned as young people who could contribute to change. To do this, she began by creating spaces or opportunities for them to take up social issues and topics that were of interest to them. This was based on a belief that "Children who learn using curriculum that is based on what matters to them are more likely to feel that what they are learning is important to their lives"(Vasquez, 2004, p. 141). While taking up these social issues and topics, Vivian made sure that children had opportunities to engage in work with real-life effects, such as doing social action projects. In this chapter, we describe one such social action project. Given this curricular orientation, Ali's response to Stefanie's comment regarding endangered animals was, therefore, no surprise. In Ali's mind, there was no doubt that she and her classmates would attempt to do something. The question was what would they do? Lee's comment "Ya. Maybe we understand, but maybe they don't understand…" speaks to the children's understanding that we each come to a situation bringing with us different perspectives and points of view that cause us to have conflicting or complementary takes on a topic, issue, or event. These differences, however, are no excuse for being a bystander. As adults, we sometimes take on a stance of sitting on the fence, thinking that doing so keeps us neutral. However, being a bystander is stance in and of itself. There is, therefore, nothing neutral about sitting on the fence, which comes with its own set of biases against what lies on the two sides of the fence.

Building from Children's Inquiry Questions

Vivian and her students had been exploring various issues regarding the environment, including endangered species. The opening conversation took place while the children were perusing fiction and nonfiction texts on the environment and rainforests and computer printouts (brought in from home by some children) pertaining to these topics. This conversation was one of many that took place during a study on critical literacy in early childhood settings that Vivian wrote about in her book, *Negotiating Critical Literacies with Young Children* (Vasquez, 2004). The more the children talked about and learned about rainforests and endangered species, the more adamant they became about finding some way to contribute to preventing the demise of such species. The result was a series of social action projects such as the creation of Travel Trunks, which we talk about in this chapter.

The Internet as Text and Tool

Along with the Travel Trunk project, in this chapter we take you to two other early childhood settings to explore various social action projects carried out by young children with the use of technology.

In this section, we focus on the use of the Internet as a text for learning about particular topics and events and the use of the Internet as a tool for use in taking social action.

Travel Trunks

The Travel Trunks project unfolded in Vivian's half-day Pre-K classroom of sixteen three- to five-year-old children in a multi-ethnic school located in a suburb of Toronto, Ontario, Canada. As noted previously, the children wanted to find some way to contribute to the preservation of endangered species.

In their attempt to do this work, Vivian and her students held a number of class meetings to brainstorm possible ideas. It was during one of these meetings that one of the children wondered whether part of the problem had to do with people not knowing enough about some of these animals. Several other children agreed that perhaps this was true. Vivian asked the children what they might do to help heighten awareness about these animals. She also asked them to think about their audience. The children decided they wanted other children in other classrooms to be their audience, hoping that those children, in turn, would also engage in a form of social action in support of endangered animals. They thought about how to make this endeavor appealing to that audience and began to explore ways that children in other classrooms might be able to connect with one another. Several children took it upon themselves to think about this as "homework." At the time, the computers available in the classroom were not connected to the Internet, so any online searches had to take place outside of the classroom. Interestingly, Vivian did not assign homework. Rather, the children took work home when they needed to find out about something to which they did not have access at school. Kohn (2007) notes,

> We should change the fundamental expectation in our schools so that students are asked to take schoolwork home only when a there's a reasonable likelihood that a particular assignment will be beneficial to most of them… The bottom line: No homework except on those occasions when it's truly necessary or when children themselves find reason to do homework to contribute to the class conversation (p. 1).

A couple of days later, the children gathered once again to share their findings, which were listed on a large sheet of chart paper. Some of these included sending informative postcards and faxing 'Did You Know…' information sheets. One of the children also talked about some research that she and her parents read about from the World Wildlife Fund (WWF) website about a sharp decrease in the tiger population. At the time (1996), the WWF was preparing to release a report on how Arctic wildlife such as polar bears were being threatened by global warming and its effects, so the group talked about this as well. Apparently if you made a donation to the WWF, you would receive a package of information and other things about the animal for which you were contributing funds.

After discussing each of the ideas and the information from the WWF, those the group felt had the most potential were circled on the chart. This short list was once again discussed. The result was the decision to create Travel Trunks: their spin on the information packets distributed by the WWF. The children made it clear that their information had to be packaged in a fun way; the children used, as an example, the small plastic bins with lids that Vivian had used to store various art supplies and writing tools. The name Travel Trunk came from a comment made by one of the children about how the bin would be like a traveling trunk for the animals. Taking this comment literally, it was decided that to make the trunks more enjoyable to use, we should include a small toy animal so the children could play with the animal they were learning about. As noted by Wohlwend (2011), "Toys represent a special kind of child-oriented text" (p. 79), which convey meanings that shift depending on the context in which it is used (Hartmann & Brougere, 2004; Brougere, 2006). The toys could, therefore, create a space for the children receiving the travel trunks to understand the animal in a way that makes sense for them. By the end of their conversation, the group had decided that the travel trunks should include the following items:

1. Small toy animal. During their class conversation, the children and Vivian decided to make different travel trunks that each focused on a particular

animal. The small toy would add an additional element of fun while the children did important work.

2. A card or Stapleless Book (see Figure 3.1) that has information about the animal and why they are in danger. The children wanted to include a card or some sort of little book of information regarding an endangered animal.

3. A note about why we made the trunk. In the note, the children wanted to share why the trunks were created. They also wanted to include a question: What will you do to help endangered animals?

4. A stamped postcard to send back to us. Vivian suggested adding the postcard because the children had asked about how they could find out what other children were going to do about endangered species. Her suggestion was to include a self-addressed postcard that could be sent back to us.

As the work on purchasing materials for the Travel Trunks began, two things became obvious. First, there was the cost involved with creating each package.

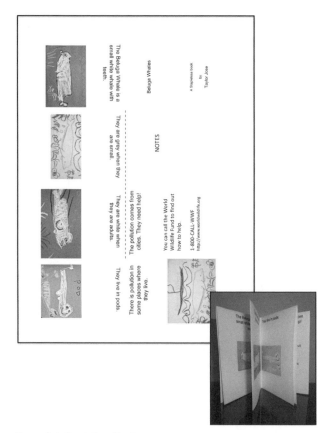

Figure 3.1 Stapleless Book

Second was the question of how to reuse the trunks so that they do not end up just sitting on a shelf somewhere once the children who receive them were done working with them. Recycling had been a topic that Vivian's class and the class next door to them had been talking about, so it was no surprise to see them engaged in such discursive exchanges. Vivian shared with them a geography project she had done with some former students whereby they sent a toy bear to a classroom not too far away from their school and then asked the children in that classroom to send the bear to yet another group of children in another school. They had wanted to see how far and where this bear would travel. With the bear, a set of self-addressed postcards were included so that whoever received the bear could send a postcard back to Vivian's class, letting them know where it had been. The children liked this idea. As a group, the class decided to create four travel trunks, each focused on one animal: polar bears, beluga whales, caribou, and ringed seals. An instruction card was then affixed to the lid of the trunk with instructions to do two things:

Resource Box 3.1

Read Write Think Stapleless Book

There is an interactive tool on the Read Write Think website located at http://www.readwritethink.org for creating stapleless books.

Using the interactive tool children can fill in the pages of an eight-paged book. Once the pages are filled you simply have to print the book and follow the instructions for folding.

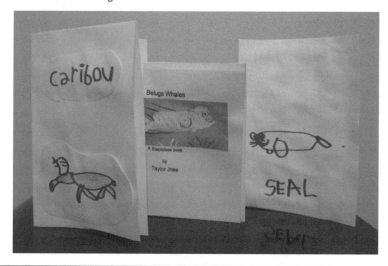

Figure 3.2 Travel Trunks

1. Send the self-addressed postcard back to the Pre-K class with a response to the question, "What will you do to help endangered animals?"
2. Send along the travel trunk to another class in another school.

At the time of this project, not many teachers were using e-mail as a means of communication, so Vivian and her students created an information sheet about the Travel Trunks and faxed those out to other Pre-K classes asking them whether they would be interested in helping get the project off the ground. They received almost immediate responses after which time the Travel Trunks were sent out. In the end, they received postcards from across Ontario, Canada and from Nova Scotia and Vancouver.

With the use of the Internet and a fax machine, Vivian and her students were able to engage in social action that had importance in their lives and for which they had great passion. As echoed repeatedly in her study on negotiating spaces for critical literacies with young children (Vasquez, 2004), this work to participate in and contribute to the world outside of school was carried out with great pleasure and in a playful but critical way. At the time of this project, technology was very limited. Even when computer access was available, the dial-up connections were extremely slow and expensive. Today, so much more could be done with access to high-speed Internet and the use of social networking tools for making information rapidly accessible to a broader audience. For instance imagine the possibilities for growing a conversation about endangered animals using a VoiceThread (see Chapter 2 for a discussion on VoiceThread) or through podcasting, which is discussed in Chapter 4 and Chapter 5.

This next classroom we enter is one brought to our attention by Mariana Souto-Manning (2012). The setting is a Pre-K classroom composed of twenty children, where the children did some work exploring sustainable communities. There was a lead teacher and an assistant teacher in the room. The children were four years old and enrolled in a full-day publicly funded program. Similar to Vivian's students, these children were also passionate about environmental issues.

Together with their teacher, the children used the Internet as a source of information and e-mail as a means of communication as they engaged in critical literacy practices (Vasquez, 2010a).

Exploring Sustainable Communities

Frustrated with the trash accumulating along the river by the playground where they played every day, a group of Pre-K students in Georgia decided to take action. However, a fence separated the playground from the river, meaning that they could not get to the trash. For safety reasons, they were not allowed to go on the other side of the fence. Rather than give up, they turned to the Internet to search for information about water use and water pollution.

Through their search, the children learned that much of the water use in the city comes from toilet flushing. To do this work, they visited sites such as the one on water usage at http://ga.water.usgs.gov/edu/wateruse.html While looking for further information regarding how to decrease the amount of water used in flushing a toilet, the children and their teacher learned of an easy and inexpensive device that could be created and inserted in toilet tanks. Sites such as *Sustainable Village* at http://www.sustainablevillage.com/node/80 or *How to Convert Any Toilet to a Low Flush Toilet* at http://www.wikihow.com/Convert-Any-Toilet-to-a-Low-Flush-Toilet, are wonderful for exploring possibilities for this kind of work. They also e-mailed experts in the world of plumbing regarding this project.

What they found is that putting a sealed plastic container filled with rocks or sand in the toilet tank helps to reduce the amount of water that is needed to flush. The children decided to use plastic icing containers from readymade icing. This way they were not only contributing to saving water, they were also engaging in recycling the food containers. After collecting a number of containers, the children filled each one with rocks. They then distributed the

Resource Box 3.2

How to Make Your Own Low Flush Toilet Device

1. Fill a plastic container with a lid that will fit in your tank (up to 0.5 gallons) with pebbles, gravel or sand.

2. Place the container in the toilet water tank.

containers to their families and community members, asking them to put the devices inside the water tank of their toilets. (See Resource Box 3.2 How to Make Your Own Low Flush Toilet Device.) According to Souto-Manning (2012), "The Internet served to democratize access of information—giving children access to the city's water use information and to possible solutions to living a more sustainable community." She further notes, "Using the Internet as a tool for change as well as e-mail as a tool for communicating with experts— both tools for critical literacy[—]the children contributed towards a more sustainable community."

The first two classroom vignettes focused on work done by children interested in dealing with global issues. In the next setting, we enter the first grade classroom of Kevan Miller where her students disrupt a longstanding school practice. Kevan's school is located just outside of Washington, DC, in a school with a very diverse student body both ethnically and economically.

Try This 3.1

Creating an Inquiry Mini-book

Using the Stapleless Book template, create an inquiry book for each of your students. You could call it a Wonderful Questions Book or an Inquiry Questions Book. Better yet, you can come up with a name for the little books with your students.

The children can then write or draw about things they are interested in learning about or exploring; their questions about the world. These can then be shared in small or large groups as a way of generating topics for study.

What's the Weather?

Kevan wrote,

> When trying to create spaces for critical literacy throughout the curriculum, I think it's helpful to notice what your students are noticing. I had been singing the weather song with my first graders since I started teaching and I never really thought much about it one way or the other.

The questions underlying Kevan's observation that she had not thought about her longstanding practice of teaching her students the weather song include What is this practice about? Why are we singing this song? Whose interests are served by singing this song? The observation is, therefore, a powerful one that indicates space is being created for change. In Kevan's case, this space opened up when one of her students asked the question, "What about other kinds of weather?" This question led to a flurry of inquiries into how weather in the area where they lived was represented and, therefore, the purpose served by the existing weather song. In another publication, Vivian writes about the process the children went through to create a new version of the song and the weather graph that went with it to provide a better representation of the weather in the area where they lived (Vasquez, 2010a).

As shown in Figure 3.3, the children noticed that the original song included only four "kinds of weather" or descriptions for weather conditions; partly cloudy, cloudy, rain, or sun. While brainstorming possible additions and deletions to the song, Kevan and her students made a list of the kinds of weather they had experienced and then voted on which weather conditions to include in the song.

Following is the revised song, which includes "two new parts" that describe a more accurate variety of weather conditions for the area where the children lived:

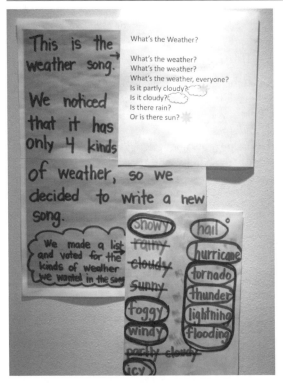

Figure 3.3 Weather Song Chart

What's the Weather—Revised

What's the weather?
What's the weather?
What's the weather, everyone?
Is it partly cloudy?
Is it cloudy?
Is there rain?
Or is there sun?
Is it snowy?
Is it foggy?
Is there wind?
Or is there ice?
Is there lightning?
Is there thunder?
A tornado?
Or a flood?

Note: The new parts of the song are italicized.

Making the Song Accessible to Others

"Let's share our song with first grade."

"No, maybe everybody. Kindergarten, 2nd, 3rd, 4th...."

"Yes, everybody!"

"How can we do that?"

"The news!"

Through various means, including the support of the Parent Teacher Association, the school had been able to maintain a broadcasting studio whereby students and teachers could create videos that could be played on television monitors in each of the classrooms. In fact, this was used for morning and afternoon announcements and/or school news. The children were used to seeing other classes sharing artwork, writing, and skits on the school's daily news program, on the TV monitors in their classrooms. Therefore, this was an obvious venue for them and a venue that they felt would make their song accessible to others. After some conversation regarding what they should do for the in-school telecast, Kevan and her students videotaped a segment that included Abha, Zahnib, and Jessica describing the original, limited version of the weather song followed by a class performance of the redesigned version of the song. It aired on the news later that week. New weather graphs were then distributed to the classes that wanted them.

Creating an opportunity for the children to redesign the weather song sent a message that texts are socially constructed with particular intent and effects on the consumer of that text. The notion of texts as socially constructed is one of the key tenets in critical literacy. This in and of itself, however, does not constitute critical literacy. However, it does create space for doing critical literacy work, such as advocating for change and understanding the points of view from which texts are created (Vasquez, 2010b). As the children problematized the weather song and chart, they did so from the point of view of children who have experienced different kinds of weather. Having experienced different kinds of weather, including flooding, for instance, helped them to read the weather song and chart as problematic because these did not represent the experiences of the children for whom they were created. With the use of a video recorder and closed circuit television, the children were able to share their story of rewriting the song and redesigning the weather graph with others in their school without having to go from room to room or without having to gather the classes together in the gymnasium or all-purpose room.

In a final reflection on this project, Kevan wrote,

There will always be other things to do, plans and obligations that compete for our attention. But what *we* attend to the *children* will attend to, so we need to be open to other ideas and alternatives. We must listen to and acknowledge the conversations in our classrooms, and make time for the opportunities that are presented to us.

REFLECTION POINT 3.1

Think about the texts that are part of your everyday routines in the classroom then ask yourself:

- For whom are these texts intended?
- What effects are intended with the use of these texts?
- What technological tools do you have in your setting?
- What might these tools afford your daily routine?

Creating Space for Social Action

In each of the classrooms we entered in this chapter, the classroom teachers created spaces for their students to engage in some form of social action. The focus of this chapter has, therefore, been on redesign as a cyclical process of exploring problematic ways of being as social constructions, deconstructing those, and then reconstructing (Janks, 2010) particular social practices to contribute to change. Further, in each of the cases, the classroom teacher used the inquiry questions of their students as the point from which to engage in this cycle. Technology was then used as a resource and communicative tool for accomplishing work that was of significance to the children.

In the next chapter, we enter the world of podcasting and consider what it affords the critical work done by a group of second grade children.

Chapter 4

Our Families Don't Understand English!

Briana: ¡Hola! Me llamo Scarlett. Puede ser que me recuerdas de la parte musical de la semana pasada. Esta semana les vamos a contar sobre como vamos a ahorrar dinero para el excursión al Acuario de Baltimore en Baltimore, Maryland, USA. Vamos a contarle el cuento de cómo vamos hacer esto.

Briana: Hi! My name is Scarlett. You might remember me from the music part last week. This week we are going to tell you about how we are raising money to go on a fieldtrip to the Baltimore Aquarium in Baltimore, Maryland, USA. We are going to tell you the story of how we are doing this.

The opening text is part of a script from the 100% Kids Podcast, an on-demand Internet broadcast that was done by Carol and Vivian in 2007 with a group of second grade children between the ages of six and eight years. Carol was the second grade classroom teacher, and Vivian was working with her to explore ways of creating spaces for critical literacies. In this chapter, we learn about the use of podcasting with a group of young children and the social action that stemmed from this work. In particular we will delve into issues of diversity and difference and language and power and how these played out as the children created their podcast. We will also share what we see as intersections between the podcasting work and critical literacies.

The setting is a large elementary school in a major metropolitan area (not too far away from Washington, DC) with approximately 900 students. It was a Title One school and a magnet school with a focus on arts and sciences. The children were from the United States, Saudi Arabia, India, Columbia, El Salvador, and Kenya. Of the twenty students in the class, fourteen were on free or reduced lunch plans. Free meal plans are made available to families who earn less than 130 percent of the poverty level whereas reduced-price meals are available to families with incomes between 130 and 185 percent of poverty level. Two families were considered homeless, which meant that according to Virginia law, these families lacked adequate and regular nighttime residence. This often meant students would have to move from house to house on an ongoing basis. Eight of the students were diagnosed with learning disabilities or in the process of being tested, and seven students participated in a gifted program.

In 2007, this diverse group of children became very interested in podcasting, when they saw Carol listening to an episode of Vivian's show, the Critical Literacy in Practice podcast, which is located at http://www.clippodcast.com. It was at that time that they began asking questions regarding podcasts and what they are. They were especially intrigued when they heard Carol's voice on one of the episodes of the Critical Literacy in Practice Podcast and wondered whether podcasting might be something they might do in their classroom.

What is a Podcast?

A podcast can be in audio and/or video format. They are often referred to as Internet broadcasts, programs, episodes, or shows that one can download and listen to using a computer or other mobile device such as an iPod Touch or Walkman. What differentiates a podcast from other audio that can be downloaded from the Internet is that they are subscribable. What this means is that anyone with Internet access can subscribe to a podcast so that when a new episode or show is available, it can automatically be delivered, or fed, to a subscriber's computer or mobile device. This happens using what is known as Really Simple Syndication, which is a method of electronically pulling (downloading) the shows from the podcast site and storing them in the browser of a computer or mobile device. You can subscribe to podcasts using a digital media player interface such as iTunes.

Creating 100% Kids

One day during a class meeting about whether to become podcasters, Carol had the children listen to a number of different online shows done by other children and adults. Figure 4.1 is a photograph of the children listening to podcasts. It did not take much time at all before the children's curiosity regarding this technological tool led them to want to try it for themselves. They decided to focus their show on various ways that they help to change inequities in their school and beyond. They wanted the topics to stem from their interests, so they decided to call it 100% Kids—a title that represents the fact that the topics and issues to be addressed in the show would come from their inquiry questions about the world around them. Figure 4.2 is an image of the podcast's homepage located at http://www.bazmakaz.com/100kids/.

Prior to beginning the work on the show, Carol and Vivian talked to the children about safety issues while surfing the net. They also talked to the children about identity issues on the Web, reminding them that in online spaces, people

Figure 4.1 Listening to Podcasts

100% KIDS is a podcast about how we are trying to help change the world ... ...with our own two hands and make it a better place for all.

We Did It and So Can You!_100%Kids_Show#8

AUDIO MP3 We Did It and So Can You [8:22m]: Play Now | Play in Popup | Download

(1758)

May 9, 2007
Dear Mrs. Felderman's Class,
Thank you for raising money
For our trip to the Baltimore
Aquarium. We appreciate
your hard work. We learned
many things and loved the
dolphin show!

Your Friends

5/8/07
Dear Mrs. Felderman's Class,
Thank you for
bringing the Aquarium
Trip back to 2nd
grade ! !

Love,
Ms. O and the Dolphins

Dear Mrs. Felderman's Class,
Our class wants to thank you for helping
us get to go to the Baltimore Aquarium.
Thanks for talking with the principal and
helping to raise money. We are excited
to go and to ride on the big bus. Thanks
again!

Love,
Mr. Miner's Class

Visitor locations

ClustrMaps

Total since 28 Feb 2007: 2,933.

Pages
» About 100% Kids

Archives
» June 2007
» May 2007
» April 2007
» March 2007
» February 2007

Figure 4.2 Podcast Homepage

can create different identities for themselves and how this creation happens through doing such things as creating radio names and personas. As such, prior to recording their first show, the children chose radio names for use in the different episodes that were different from their own names. The names used throughout this chapter and the next chapter are the children's self-selected radio names.

Some of the topics the children addressed during the show were global warming, animal rights, and other equity issues at school. In this chapter, we focus on Subrina, one of the girls in Carol's class who suggested that the show needed to be in Spanish because many of the "families don't understand English." In fact, more than half of the children's families, including Subrina's, did not speak English as their first language. The issue of for whom the podcast was accessible was one the children had not previously considered. Once the concern was raised, several students immediately volunteered to help make the podcast in "their language." The conversation went farther as the children realized there are other home languages, such as Arabic and Urdu, that were also pushed aside by an English-only curriculum and that those languages also needed to be respected in the show. This was a significant literacy moment for the class as they took up the issue of access and domination; who has access to the podcast, which language was most dominant, and in what ways. Janks (2010), talks about this in her seminal work, *Literacy and Power*, and asks "How does one provide access to dominant forms while at the same time valuing and promoting the diverse languages and literacies of our students and in the broader society?" (p. 24)

Janks (2010) points out "many languages don't have a word for literacy" (p.1), and yet the word in its English form is used in some countries where a literal translation does not exist. This speaks to the privileged use of the English language and the importance of creating space in the classroom curriculum for addressing the issue of linguistic and cultural diversity.

Within a critical literacy framework, teachers address issues of social justice and equity that arise from the social and political conditions in the communities where students live (Comber, 2001; Vasquez, 2004, 2010c). What this meant for the students' experiences, activities, and curriculum was that the issues and topics for discussion came from the children and what they saw as important in their lives and their communities. By putting the children and their concerns and questions at the center of the curriculum, the children and teacher co-construct a critical curriculum that allows for social issues and issues of equity to be authentically and purposefully addressed.

Introducing Subrina

Subrina was born in Guatemala and moved to the United States with her family when she was five years old. She lived with her mother and her baby sister in an apartment next to the school. During the school year, Subrina and her family moved three times within the neighborhood. Her family's final move during

Try This 4.1

Observation Chart

One of the questions often asked of us by teachers is, "How do you find out what topics are of interest to children?" Through the years, we each have learned that we needed to listen differently to the children's conversations not only during such times as class meetings or book discussions but as they worked in various areas of the classroom; while playing dress-up, while building structures, while in the playground. As we listened, we did so with an ear for the underlying social issues embedded in their talk and play.

When Vivian was a preschool teacher one of the ways she kept track of these issues was using post it notes. What she did was to jot down notes on individual post-it pieces throughout the day and then affix these on a chart labeled with the children's names.

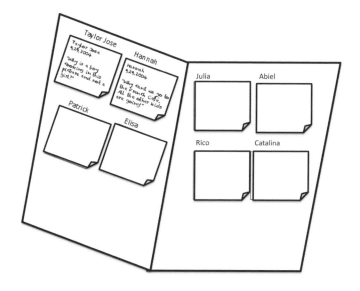

the school year was to a room in an apartment that was rented to them by a classmate's family. Title 42, Chapter 119, Subchapter I, of the United States Code, defines being homeless as an individual who lacks a fixed, regular, and adequate nighttime residence (from http://portal.hud.gov/portal/page/portal/HUD). Based on this definition, Subrina and her family were homeless.

She began her schooling at Stapler Elementary in kindergarten and, as of this writing, she had graduated from fifth grade and the school. She had many friends although she played primarily with her close friend Amy. Subrina and her family moved in with Amy's family at the end of the school year. Subrina often found herself involved in discussions about who she was or was not friends with, but she usually found her own ways to maintain her friendships. Her attentiveness to social dynamics was evident through her efforts with nurturing friendships and helping to solve classroom concerns.

Subrina was always proud to talk about her family and speak in Spanish. One of her favorite school activities was the Spanish Reading Club that met after school once a week. There she was able to participate in reading, writing, and singing activities in Spanish. The goal of the club was to provide a place for Spanish-speaking children to maintain and further their use of their first language. Subrina's love for her family and pride in her first language and community became evident with her push to include Spanish translations in the podcast.

Exclusion and Inclusion

While reflecting on the issue raised by the children, Carol wrote the following in her journal:

> I was not sure how we would be able to best translate our shows into the many languages spoken in our class, but I could not overlook how cognizant the children were about how people would not be able to understand their podcast if we did not include translations. As I did with many situations that confronted our class that were difficult, I provided space for the children to share their ideas. I made sure to emphasize to the children that I only understood English and French, so my assistance would be limited. The children began counting those in the class who spoke English and some children volunteered to write scripts in Spanish. The children told me "not to worry" because Senora Duarte spoke Spanish, so she could take my place during the "Spanish parts."
>
> At the time of this discussion, I began to think about the other languages spoken by the families in our class such as Arabic and Urdu—How could we have those languages included as well? I remembered Lucy, one of the students and Mr. A, the PE teacher, developing a growing relationship that was predominantly carried out in Arabic. They could speak Arabic on the show. For the two girls who spoke Urdu, one of the girls said that her mom could help us. The class was overwhelmed by excitement with the children's side discussions about how they could get "their languages" on the podcast.

In the days that followed, Carol began to realize that translating the show into different languages would be quite a challenge. Most significant was that many of the children could speak a language other than English, but they were unable to read or write in that language. At the same time, some of them expressed feeling too shy to speak "their language" on the show regardless of what language it was.

While raising the concern that people who spoke languages other than English would not be able to understand the podcast, Subrina brought to the fore an issue that was socially significant (Vasquez, 2004) to her and many of her classmates. Doing so created an opportunity for the children to take on the position of "agents, developing a feeling of self that if one acts in a certain manner and acts strategically, certain goals can be reached" (Souto-Manning and Felderman, 2012). In this case,

> recognition of the various languages of the class and their families brought attention to a larger issue of who would be able to listen and understand the shows and the messages the children shared through the podcast. The children's awareness of who would be excluded was clearly present (Souto-Manning and Felderman, 2012).

Although they were not able to translate the show into multiple languages, they were at least able to make the podcast more accessible to the Spanish-speaking members of the school community by including sections translated into that language. In doing so, the children's awareness of audience was expanded to include notions of access, domination, diversity, and privilege. An audience was no longer just a group of people reading, viewing, or listening to a text. Rather, audience became a much more complex body located in time and space. While continuing to talk about how to make their show accessible to as many diverse people as possible, they discussed the ways in which privileged community practices, such as speaking English as a dominant language, advantages certain audiences while disadvantaging others. In this way, they were able to explore what Janks (2010) refers to as the relationship between language and power. As a result, the children definitely grew in their understanding that their listening audiences may understand a language different from their own. "They became aware of the ways in which employing English only excluded many and reaffirmed their resolve to put together more inclusive podcasts" (Souto-Manning and Felderman, 2012).

Negotiating Identities and Growing Literacies

Both Carol and Subrina's former teachers had always worried about her as she struggled in reading, writing, and math. Academically, Subrina was on the at-risk list and had been since kindergarten. Children were labeled at-risk when their reading, writing, and math work was not on grade level—based on district standards—at the end of the school year. Children seen to be at risk more than often are the children who are defined as learning-disabled. As such, from the start, Carol had begun putting together artifacts of Subrina's learning as the initial step toward identifying Subrina as having learning disabilities.

When the podcast work began in January of second grade, Subrina was assessed by Carol to be reading almost at an end-of-first-grade level. She was, therefore, about half a year behind her peers. Her writing work was at a beginning first grade level, but her oral and listening skills were on grade level as was much of her math work. Subrina was a B1 level (just above beginner according to the school district) English-language learner, although she had been in an English-speaking school for two-and-a-half years. Her slow progress in English acquisition was another reason she was placed on the at-risk list. Subrina could not read or write in her first language of Spanish, either but, as mentioned earlier, she was part of the Spanish reading and writing club offered by the school to assist children in maintaining fluency in their home language. Nevertheless, Subrina participated often in class discussions, and she asked many questions. In spite of her struggles with academics, she regularly shared that she loved coming to school. By the end of the school year, as we completed the final 100% Kids episode, Sabrina had missed the grade level benchmark set by the district by only a few points. This was an incredible accomplishment that Carol believes was aided in part by the confidence she gained from performing literacy while podcasting.

While podcasting, Subrina was able to tell stories that have significance for her in the same way that Vasquez's (2004) preschool students were able to do while taking social action to change inequitable school practices in their setting. Feeling personally invested in her learning kept her in the game in spite of the increasing difficulty (Vasquez, 2010b) involved with researching, reading, writing, and performing scripts for a podcasting audience.

Following is a transcript from the opening segment of one episode. The opening piece was considered an honor for the students because it often set the tone for the show. For some, this was the most challenging segment because it often involved unscripted conversation. The children had deliberately chosen to leave the opening segment less formal as a way to attract their audience and make them feel as though they could be part of the conversation. Even if the segment is unscripted, the children had to do some background research on various topics included in the opening piece. They then had to recall that background information while recording. For Subrina, participating in the opening of the show was most exciting and she accepted the challenge with fervor.

Amy: Hi, my name is Amy and welcome to the opening of our show.
Subrina: Hi, my name is Subrina. Today we are going to talk about endangered animals.
Hannah: Welcome, I am Hannah, and we are talking about the animals in danger of dying.

Amy:	Maybe we need to have some good zoos to help protect them. We are going to the zoo in April, and we want to talk with the zookeepers.
Subrina:	Some animals are dying because they don't have food. People are cutting down the plants and trees that animals eat.
Emma:	The animals and trees are important to the world because they give food and air to make us live. One way we can help is to plant more trees and plants. Me and my dad are planting tomatoes.
Subrina:	My dad is planting a lot of apple trees and other trees. These trees will help us, the animals, and the world. I like apples; so does Emma and Amy.
Emma:	No, I don't like them, I love them!!
Amy and Subrina:	Us too!

In this exchange, Subrina talks about what she has learned about why some animals are in danger: because "people are cutting down plants and trees" that are their food source. She also shares an example through personal experience of the sort of action that needs to be taken to change this problematic situation: planting more trees.

The flow of the informal conversation in the previous exchange demonstrates Subrina's degree of comfort with engaging in conversation for the show. This enthusiastic participation in a school event was not previously a characteristic Carol would have associated with her. Experiences such as these were instrumental in helping Carol recognize Subrina's strengths making it much easier to support her as a literacy learner. Previous to the show, Subrina was not as comfortable or confident to share what was on her mind, nor was she willing to participate in the literacy work done in the classroom. The podcast seemed to provide her with a unique and purposeful place to be a reader, writer, and storyteller—a new identity through which she more readily accessed the curriculum. The more she podcasted, the more her identity as a confident podcaster began to flow into other parts of the school day.

Carol reflected,

> I have to admit that I worried about Subrina…because of how nervous she gets. She told me that she messed up once "but it was okay." This relaxed response meant a lot for me to hear as I think about her as a learner and as she said the words, her whole body stood tall and she had a truly confident smile on her face. No one spoke for her as she explained how well her group's recording session went. I felt like today there was a great spark in her confidence as a reader, writer, and speaker.
>
> I noted in my journal that I believed Subrina would be highly motivated to push herself and her efforts in reading and writing for the podcast.

Typically excited about school, I saw her excitement towards the podcast as infectious and a way to get other children who were more hesitant to regard the podcast as safe or "ok." Subrina also enjoyed doing activities with her classmates that involved an element of pretend. In this sense, I saw the act of using a microphone to record her work as a specific motivator since it (allowed her to be a) "rock star" or "celebrity."

I saw some of the kids come to life in a different way as they imitated their favorite TV stars (Hannah Montana, characters from "the Suite Life") and music artists (Britney Spears) when they practiced holding a microphone. Subrina particularly came to life as a "TV news reporter." Most of all, she used the time to talk with her friends in Spanish. Seeing Subrina use the microphone opportunity to use her first language caught on quickly with other classmates who spoke a language other than English as their first language.

Creating New Spaces for Participation

For Carol's second graders, podcasting became a new means for accessing and participating in school. This was true for native English speakers and for English-language learners. Nixon and Gutierrez (2008) note that in many traditional classrooms, play and the use of imagination with younger grades is often dismissed or included in a way that is over-structured. They believe that the use of play in the classroom is especially important for English learners as it affords them time to participate in learning environments that are not part of scripted learning models such as readiness programs. Further, Nixon and Gutierrez (2008) believe that such play and participation in imaginary worlds "can support learning and development by changing how individuals see the world, how they act in the world, and how they think about possibilities for the future" (p. 125). Participating in the podcast created spaces for students such as Subrina to see the world of the classroom differently, thereby encouraging her to position herself differently among her classmates within the curriculum and with her teacher. Creating new identities through podcasting created opportunities for the children to play and use their imaginations as they constructed and produced the show each week. Following is an outline of the schedule they created for themselves.

Mondays

On Monday, Carol and the children would begin the week by listening to a newly released episode and then begin planning for the upcoming show. This meant figuring out what topics, issues, and events to include in each segment. These included an opening/introduction, dedication, news, jokes, music, and other pieces that the children felt needed to be added from week to week. Segments would then be assigned to different groups of students.

Tuesday to Thursday

During the week, the children would spend time researching their topics, gathering information for their segments, writing and rehearsing scripts, and making any changes to the program.

Friday

On Fridays, Vivian would come in to record the audio. She would then take the audio files home, edit them based on the children's requests for certain music and sound effects between segments, and release the show on Monday morning.

At first, the podcasting work was done during Carol's language arts block in the morning. However, as Carol realized the cross-curricular work that resulted from podcasting, she allocated more and more time throughout the day for creating the show. In some ways, the podcasting work became a tool for seamlessly integrating learning across the various content areas.

The Final Show

Subrina's part in the final show demonstrated her growth in confidence with reading, writing, and participating in literacy activities she previously shied away from:

> Subrina: Hi my name is Subrina. We want to talk about the end of school and how we are moving schools and different houses. We are so sad we are leaving because we love our bestest friends who always take care of us. We will miss them on the last day of school SO MUCH because we love each other a lot.

At the start of the school year, love would not have been a word Carol would have associated with Subrina and her feelings for anything having to do with school. In time, and especially as a result of her participation in the 100% Kids Podcast, there was no doubt in Carol's mind that indeed Subrina meant every word.

Try This 4.2

Try Podcasting With Your Students

Have you thought about podcasting with your students? Here are some other ways teachers and their students have used podcasting in their settings. Consider trying out one of these ideas in your classroom:

- Creating descriptions for art work done in the classroom
- Reflecting on field trips or excursions
- Reflecting on local happenings
- Book talks or book reviews
- Sharing ideas about particular topics, issues, or events.

Children's Construction of Identity

Studies of children's construction of identities have come to the forefront recently (Gee, 2003; Marsh, 2005; Vasquez, 2010a). This work is about who children are, how they see themselves, how they position themselves, how they are seen and positioned by others, who they think they can be based on the messages they encounter in the world, and who they want to be in the world. Such work embraces the complexity of children's everyday lives particularly as they navigate daily experiences at home, school, and other social places. Subrina experienced first-hand the transformative effects of being able to negotiate an identity through podcasting. Her newfound confidence helped her to speak up and problematize the podcast's lack of accessibility for non-English speakers. In doing so, she helped punctuate the unintended message sent out to families who were non-English speakers that they needed to speak English if they wanted to fully participate in the children's podcast. Languages other than English were not considered until Subrina brought her concern to the class's attention. This example of Subrina's making a case for why the podcast ought to be done in different languages provides insight into how bringing the children's interests and backgrounds into the curriculum raises awareness of important social issues that so easily could be swept under the rug.

REFLECTION POINT 4.1

What sorts of possibilities for connecting with the world outside the classroom are made available through the use of podcasting and, specifically, how might this tool be used in carrying out critical literacy work in your setting?

How might this social media tool work to position children differently, creating space for them to participate differently in different spaces and places?

In the next chapter, we continue to explore the use of podcasting with young children as we re-enter Carol's second grade classroom to learn about what happened when the worlds of social studies, critical literacy, and podcasting intersect.

Resource Box 4.1

 Podcasting Sites

Having young children listen to various podcasts from around the globe that focus on different issues and events is one way of helping them experience the notion that texts are socially constructed. Accompanying conversations could focus on the ways in which the podcasters offer particular perspectives on the issues and events they describe and that those perspectives are shaped by their experiences both in and outside school and by the resources that have been available to them. Part of this conversation could also focus on how a listener interprets or makes sense of the podcasts they hear or watch based on their own experiences and the resources that have been available to them.

Following is a small sampling of podcasts.

- Allanah's Appleby Showcase
  http://allanah.podomatic.com/
  A podcast created by a group of Year Four (eight-year-old) children in Nelson, New Zealand who were learning new ways of communicating.
- Critical Literacy in Practice Podcast
  http://www.clippodcast.com
  A podcast hosted by Vivian Vasquez that focuses on critical literacy as it is practiced and talked about in different spaces and places.
- The SG Show
  http://sgshow.blogspot.com/
  Sam and his dad, Steve, talk about books, fun things for families to do together, and, life in general from their home in California, USA. We would recommend listening to the earlier shows (2005–2008) that were recorded when Sam was in first grade to third grade.
- YO-HO from Yokosuka
  http://learninginhand.com/storage/ourcity/yokosuka/index.html
  This podcast was done by a group of second grade students in Yokosuka, Japan for Our City Podcast produced by Tony Vincent (http://learninginhand.com/OurCity/). The show focuses on people, places and things in Japan.
- 100% Kids Podcast
  http://www.bazmakaz.com/100kids/
  A podcast on social issues and events that of importance to a group of second grade students in Virginia, USA.

Resource Box 4.2

 Resources on Podcasting and Young Children

Vasquez, V. (2010). A podcast is born: Critical literacy and new technologies. In V. Vasquez (Ed.). *Getting Beyond I Like the Book: Creating Spaces for Critical Literacy in K-6 Classrooms.* Newark, DE: International Reading Association.

Vasquez, V. (2010). iPods, puppy dogs, and podcasts: Imagining literacy instruction for the 21st century. *School Talk,* 15(2), 1–2.

Vasquez, V., & Harste, J. C. (2010). Kid-watching, negotiating, and podcasting: Imagining literacy instruction for the 21st century. In Association of Literacy Educators and Researchers (Eds., pp. 17–30) *Building Literacy Communities: Yearbook 32 of the Association of Literacy Educators and Researchers.* Arlington, TX: Texas A&M University.

Resource Box 4.3

 How to Podcast

There are four main things you will need to do a podcast once you have come up with the topic or issue that you want to communicate to others.

1. A recording device
   To record your audio, you will need either a computer with a built-in mic or mic you can attach or a digital recording device. For the 100% Kids podcast, we used one of two mics pictured below.

iRiver and microphone   Zoom H2

2. Software to edit your audio
   Whether you want to edit your recordings is up to you. Some podcasters use software built into their computers or available

for free download from the Internet. The most common would be Garageband for Mac users and Audacity for PC users. Other podcasters simply post the audio as recorded. The only thing you will need to ensure is that you save your recording as an mp3 file.

Some recorders can be set up to record in mp3 format. We would recommend you use such a recorder if you are not interested in editing your audio. However, if you are interested in editing your audio, you can go to the Web site of the editing software you are using for instructions regarding that process.

3. A place to host your audio

Once you have recorded your audio, you will need a place to host it. First, you will need to decide on who your audience will be. Will you make the podcast available to the general public or only to your school community? If you want to make your podcast available to an audience beyond your school community, you can use a paid hosting service such as Libsyn (www.libsyn.com) or GoDaddy (www.godaddy.com). The cost for hosting is very reasonable, starting at approximately $4.99 a month. These hosting sites provide instructions regarding how to upload files.

If you plan to make your show available to only your school community, you can host it on your local network the same way that you would other files. You will simply have to add a hyperlink to the location where you save it.

4. A place to post your audio

The final step in the process is to post your audio to an online space so that it is accessible to others. There are numerous hosting sites available if you choose to make your podcast available to an audience beyond your school community. The 100% Kids episodes are posted using Wordpress blogging software. It uses Wordpress for its homepage. Blogger (http://www.blogger.com) or Go Daddy (http://www.godaddy.com) are two sites often used by podcasters for creating their podcast homepage. What you would do is create your audio, upload it to your audio hosting site (see No. 3), and then link that audio on the podcasting homepage site.

If you choose to keep your podcast on your school's server, you will need to see what is available at your school.

There are also numerous Web sites and videos on Youtube that take you through the recording and editing process step by step. Following are some search terms you can use to locate these sites: how to podcast, podcast hosting, editing a podcast, what is a podcast. Podcast411, located at http://www.podcast411.com/, also has some nice tutorials on audio podcasting.

Chapter 5

What about Antarctica?

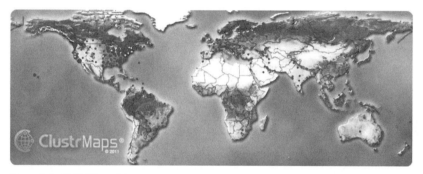

Figure 5.1 CLIP Clustr Map

During one of our planning meetings for the podcast, the children spent time looking through the website of Vivian's critical literacy podcast (described in Chapter 4) and noticed what they described as an error. The children were carefully viewing Vivian's podcast homepage to make decisions regarding what they wanted to include on their site. They looked at the banner across the top of the screen that held the title of the broadcast, noticing how the words and images were organized. They looked at the colors she had chosen for the banner, the background for the webpage, and the various headings throughout the site. The children noticed she had links to other podcasts and websites to the left and right sides of the page, which led listeners to more information about the topics discussed on her podcast. They wondered what kinds of effects each of these elements would have on someone viewing the site. Last, the children noticed there is a map on the site with red dots on it (see Figure 5.1 The Clustr Map on the Critical Literacy in Practice Podcast site. Also refer to Resource Box 5.1 for information regarding free software such as the Clustr Map for use on Web sites). Carol explained to the class that it was a map of the world like the map in their classroom. She told them the dots represent the listeners from countries around the world who are visiting the podcast site. As they looked closer, they observed that the dots were different sizes. Carol explained that the size of the dots represented a certain number of people listening or viewing from a particular place. For example, the smallest dot would represent a cluster of one to nine people or visits to the site whereas the largest dot would represent more than 1,000 visitors to the site. The children were impressed with how many "dots" there were on Vivian's map and how they were all spread out across different continents. As the children looked more closely at the map one of them asked, "What about Antarctica?"

In this chapter, we continue to explore the children's use of podcasting. This time, however, we focus on the children's work on deconstructing an online text. Specifically, we describe and analyze what happened after the "What about Antarctica?" question was posed.

Reading the Clustr Map

At first, the children thought there had been an oversight. Their initial reaction was to let Vivian know that her map was incorrect and that, "…the makers of the map forgot to put in Antarctica…." The children felt a sense of urgency and wanted to get in touch with Vivian right away. In support of their needs, Carol took her laptop, sat on the floor with the group, and together they began composing an email:

> Date: Mon., Feb 12, 2007 at 10:12 am
> Subject: Antarctica
> To: Vivian Vasquez
>
> Dear Vivian,
> All of us in our 2nd grade class are looking at your podcast site. We noticed on your map of the world that Antarctica is missing. Do you think there are listeners there?
> Love,
>
> Stapler's M-1
> 2nd grade

In the children's e-mail, they ask, "Do you think there are listeners there?" Carol's students had some sense of the real-world effects of texts; in particular, they worried about how the exclusion of Antarctica on the map positioned those who may be listeners coming from that area. They had begun to wonder about the effects of text when they were looking closely at Vivian's podcast homepage, where they wondered what the advantages or disadvantages were of adding different elements to a Web site. At that time, they wondered about the effects of things that an audience could see. Now they wondered about the effects of something that was not visible. In essence, they were asking the critical question: Who is left out and, therefore, who is disadvantaged?

As the children continued to have a discussion about the missing continent, the conversation shifted from a statement regarding Vivian's map of the world being inaccurate to a question: What message does this omission send to her listeners in Antarctica? Central to their concerns were, therefore, issues of access (to the technology) and positioning (leaving out residents of Antarctica).

Part of the second grade social studies curriculum involved being able to use maps, including knowing and being able to locate the seven continents of the world. The observation of the map was, therefore, significant for the class and their social studies curriculum for second grade. As the children's teacher, Carol was pleased about her students' observation because it demonstrated their understandings of the continents and where they are on a map. However, even more exciting was the children's concern for the real-world effects of leaving Antarctica off the map because she felt this took their learning to a more critical place. They saw leaving the continent off the map as "unfair" because, they said, leaving it off made it seem as though "the continent did not exist." They lamented: "..the people there could be forgotten." The observation created space for conversations about what Janks (2010) refers to as the politics of inclusion and exclusion.

The children were very excited to receive a response from Vivian addressing their concerns for her map:

From: Vivian Vasquez
Date: Tues, Feb 13, 2007 at 10:00 am
Subject: Antarctica

What an excellent question. I think I will write to the Clustr map folks to ask them about "missing" Antarctica or if you would rather do it then please feel free to act on this.
Can't wait to see you.

Vivian

The advantage of access to e-mail was that they could engage in this exchange more rapidly than if they had to wait for Vivian's next visit to their classroom. Vivian's prompt response demonstrated her genuine interest in their concern and that she takes their interests and questions very seriously. She also acknowledged the importance of their question. By writing "I think I will write to the Clustr map folks to ask them about missing Antarctica," she demonstrates to the children a possible next step to get more information about the map. Further, Vivian makes clear that she is confident the children can take action themselves when she states, "…if you would rather do it then please feel free to act on this." With this, the children were encouraged to keep this line of inquiry going.

In her reflection journal Carol wrote,

What stood out to me more than to the students in Vivian's e-mail was her statement to the children "to act" on the problem. Vivian's background with critical literacy and her work to use literacy to take action, were evident in her word choice. Her response modeled the use of letter writing to take action as well as reinforced to the children that their first step in e-mailing/writing the letter to her was already taking an active part in searching for information, creating awareness of a problem, and ultimately, taking a part in making a change.

Moments after Vivian's response, her husband, who had worked with Vivian on editing the children's audio, also responded to the children's concern:

From: Andy Bilodeau
Date: Tues, Feb 13, 2007 at 10:15 am
Subject: Antarctica

Hello Stapler's M-1 2nd Grade Class
I actually have an answer to your question about the lack of Internet traffic on the CLIP map for Antarctica. It seems that the Internet connection in the Antarctic is very very slow...in fact they are only able to get "dial-up" speeds. This means that they can only have enough bandwidth to be able to check e-mail and are not able to use a browser to visit any websites like the CLIP website.

In fact, a fellow podcaster was asking us podcasters to send CDs and MP3 files to the only radio station in Antarctica so that the people living down in Antarctica could have something to listen to.

Andy's response gave the children one possible answer to their question about the missing continent and an idea of how they could get their podcast to Antarctica so the people there would be able to listen to their show. Although the children continued to worry about listeners from Antarctica, they did not pursue the issue farther as they instead prepared scripts for upcoming episodes for their show.

Further Explorations

Clearly, much more could have been done with regard to this issue. For instance, Carol could have done an inquiry into critical cartography with the children whereby they might have discovered that Antarctica is cropped off maps more often than we realize. As the people at Clustr Maps did not respond to Vivian's queries, all we can do is come up with possible interpretations. One interpretation is what Andy suggested; Antarctica is deliberately left off due to lack of bandwidth. Another interpretation could be that the Clustr map uses what is referred to as a Mercator projection, a navigation tool developed in the 1500s by a man named Geradus Mercator, which consisted of a rectangular grid with lines of latitude and longitude. According to the information on Web sites such as http://www.petersmap.com and http://odtmaps.com, the Mercator projection creates distortions that increase in size as you move away from the equator. The closer you get to the poles, the greater the distortion. As a result of severe distortion at the poles, it is common to crop Antarctica off the map. Sometimes a brief notation regarding this appears on a map. If the children had learned about this, they might have suggested for the folks at Clustr maps to add such a notation when maps are created or to use a different projection, one that includes Antarctica. There are some very good resources available at the ODT Maps Web site located at http://odtmaps.com. The National Geographic Web site also has some interesting resources with regard to this available online at http://shop.nationalgeographic.com.

REFLECTION POINT 5.1

For some time, it has been known that the widely used Mercator map distorts the size of landmasses. Yet, the map is often used uncontested. At one point in time, when most of the world powers were European, this map, with Europe at the center, could have provided a convenient and psychologically practical way to convey domination. The result is a Euro– and North America–centric worldview. Was this intentional? Maybe so, maybe not. The more important question is why is the map still so widely recognized and used? While reflecting on this, consider our own school practices and the ways in which we sometimes engage in teaching practices that are not as useful to or considerate of the students in our classrooms

Every Map Takes a Point of View

With young children, an exploration into the social construction of maps would be a powerful activity that would help them to understand that all texts are created with particular intent and that these texts have particular effects on the reader or consumer of that text. As noted by Wood and Kaiser (2001), "every map takes a point of view" (p. 12). The point of view from which a map is created results in the inclusion of some things and the exclusion of other things. As in any text, what you do not see, what is left off the page, is equally as important as what is included. One way to have children experience point of view is to have them create a map of the school neighborhood from different perspectives: mail carrier, crossing guard, environmentalist, architect; what would each of these people want to see on a map? What things would matter to them and why? What things would put them at an advantage? What things would put them at a disadvantage? Resource Box 5.2 includes a number of Web sites that children can visit to view a diverse variety of maps. There is also information there regarding how to receive a set of map postcards for free. Google Earth located at http:// www.google.com also is a terrific online tool for studying space and place. They even have a specific site for educators located at http://sitescontent.google.com/ google-earth-for-educators/. With this software, you and your students are able to view maps from all over the world in 3-D or in street view. You can explore landscapes; you can measure buildings and mountains and draw directly on the maps with a drawing tool. You can also map out tours of various spaces and places to share with one another. For some cities, historical imagery is available so that you can see what particular places looked like throughout different periods in time. Most of the resources on the site are available for free. They also have a grant for which you can apply to receive access to more advanced applications.

REFLECTION POINT 5.2

- What are some other things we might have done from a critical literacy perspective using technology to further explore the issue of access?
- What other kinds of work with maps might we have done to explore the issue of inclusion and exclusion further?

The 100% Kids Clustr Map

In spite of the issues the children had with the map, they wanted to add one to their podcast Web site so they too could document and learn where their listeners lived in the world. The children checked on the Clustr Map regularly, excited to see the dots growing in size and spreading to different parts of the world. The children often wondered who lived in the different states and countries that were dotted on the map. Sometimes they waited in anticipation for dots to appear where relatives or friends of their families said they would tune in to the show. As many of the children had immigrated to the United States with their families, those children were quick to show one another where "their countries" were on the map, with many of them hoping that a dot would appear. As they did this, stories were often told of times gone by. Comber (2012) notes that working on local history is sometimes taken up by middle school teachers to reconnect students with their communities, but it is rarely explored in early childhood classrooms. She continues by saying that young children are often treated as ahistorical subjects, and "...people with little history themselves and little understanding of history, excepting of course their assumed fascination with prehistory in terms of dinosaurs" (2012, p. 343). However, there are studies that show the ways in which young children are able to work with narratives of their past as a cultural resource in support of their learning (Comber, 2003; Uprichard, 2008). In Carol's case, engaging in place-based pedagogies was not her initial intent, but creating spaces for critical literacies resulted in the possibility of doing such work. In a way the Clustr map served as an artifact, an object through which some of the children were able to share stories of their lives, including family stories related to places from which their families emigrated and where they still had family members residing. Pahl and Rowsell (2010) state, "Identities reside on a sea of stuff and experiences" (p.8), and such was the case with the map, which evoked stories that the children may not have previously shared with one another. As they did this, relationships changed as they got to know one another in new and different ways. The podcast also changed, as discussed in Chapter 4, with the addition of episodes that were done in two languages, English and Spanish.

Columbia Gets a Dot

The children took it upon themselves to transfer the information from the Clustr Map to the wall map in their classroom. They used post-it notes to keep track of where their listeners lived. This led to a host of lessons about the continents, countries, and states. The children sometimes went online searching for information on some of the countries that were unfamiliar to them. The children also wondered why they did not have listeners in some areas including the countries where some of their families lived. The day that Columbia appeared dotted on the map was, therefore, a day of celebration. Scarlett and Martha were particularly thrilled as both their families were from Columbia. Martha, who was a quiet student, began to talk about her grandparents who lived in Columbia and how she could not go there to see them. She shared life stories about times spent with them. She continued to talk about how much she loved her grandparents and how much they loved her but that her family did not get to see them much at all. Scarlett shared similar stories about her family.

At the end of the school year, Martha's mother came up to us and shared that her parents were the ones in Columbia. With tears in her eyes, she told us how expensive it was to connect long distance with them. She said that each week, Martha's grandparents would go to a place where they could access a computer and listen to the children's show so that they could hear their granddaughter's voice and hear about what she was learning in school in America. Martha's mother thanked us for creating a space, through the podcast, in which their family could connect. This was more than we had ever thought could happen. From the onset of the project, we knew the children would be reaching a new audience through the use of technology, but we did not realize the potential of podcasting as a tool for connecting families across time and space and that it could lead to exploring pedagogies of place.

Carol

> After the school year ended and into the next year I continued to check the podcast to see how many people still listened and where they lived. What again struck me was how many new dots were on the map of the children's home countries. Many of the children went home to be with other members of their families over the summer, so they showed their families what they did in school. Some of the families moved back to their home countries, so I saw their "dots," too.

Comber (2001) asserts that early childhood education often positions young children as innocent and naïve. On the contrary, she suggests that young children are "only too aware of what's fair, what's different, who gets the best deal… long before they start school" (Comber, 2001, p. 5). They learn these lessons from everyday life as they navigate the various spaces and places that they inhabit. Such was the case with Carol's students as demonstrated in this chapter and the previous one.

In the next chapter, we move out of a traditional school setting and enter into a world of co-op learning where parents and teachers work together on various projects.

Resource Box 5.1

 Free Software for Use on Web sites/ Blogs/ Podcast Sites

- Clustr Map
http://www.clustrmaps.com/
Uses mapping software to keep track of visitors to your podcast or Web site
- Flickr
http://www.flickr.com/
Photo sharing site
- Google Analytics
http://www.google.com/analytics/
Provides informational data on your website traffic
- YouTube
http://www.youtube.com/
Site for watching and posting original videos
- Googlemaps
http://maps.google.com/
Allows you to add maps to your homepage
- Twitter
https://twitter.com/
Instant updates from whomever you friend on Twitter

Resource Box 5.2

Free Map Postcards

Send a stamped self-addressed No. 10 envelope to ODT and they will send you samples of their map postcards, including the Population Map, Peters Map, Mecca-centered Azimuthal projection, and Waterman Butterfly Map. Mail to: ODT, PO Box 134, Amherst MA 01004. International customers please be sure to apply sufficient postage for 1 oz. first-class mail.

 ### Other Map Resources

- Background on Hobo-Dyer Map http://odtmaps.com/behind_the_maps/hobo-Dyer_map/default.asp
- Mercator Map of the World http://www.public.asu.edu/~aarios/resourcebank/maps/page10.html
- Peter's Map of the World http://cartography-huber.com/p42/the-peters-world-map
- Polyhedral Maps http://www.progonos.com/furuti/MapProj/Normal/ProjPoly/projPoly.html
- What's Behind the Maps? http://odtmaps.com/behind_the_maps/
- McArthur's Corrective Map of the World http://www.odt.org/pictureembed.htm

 ### Readings about Using Maps in Educational Settings

Alibrandi, M. (2003). What's GIS done for me lately? In *GIS in the Classroom: Using Geographic Information Systems in Social Studies and Environmental Science* (pp. 1–17). Portsmouth, NH: Heinemann.

Kaiser, W., & Wood, D. (2001). *Seeing through Maps: The Power of Images to Shape Our World View.* Amherst, MA: ODT, Inc.

Segall, A. (2003, September/October). Maps as stories about the world. *Social Studies and the Young Learner, 16*(1), 21–25.

Sobel, D. (1998). The geography of childhood: A developmental portrait. In *Mapmaking with Children: Sense of Place Education for Elementary Years* (pp. 10–23). Portsmouth, NH: Heinemann.

Try This 5.1

Playing With Maps

Show your students two different maps selected from the Web sites in Resource Box 5.2 and ask them what they notice. There are no right or wrong answers, just different possible observations.

Then show them McArthur's Universal Corrective Map of the World from one of Web sites listed below, and tell them the story of twelve-year-old Stuart McArthur.

Stuart McArthur lived in Melbourne, Australia. When he was twelve years old, he drew his first version of the Universal Corrective Map of how he saw the world to be. When his teacher saw the map, she made him do it again saying that his map was wrong. When he was fifteen years old, his parents sent him to school in Japan where his American classmates made fun of him. They teased him and told him he was from the bottom of the world. This angered Stuart so much that he promised himself that one day he would publish a map with Australia at the top of the world map. Years later, in 1979, while he was at Melbourne University, he created the world's first modern map with Australia at the top. Now his map is sold in lots of places around the world.

Have your students create their own maps of the school or the neighborhood after viewing different maps from Resource Box 5.2. When they are done creating their maps, ask them to talk about how they came to create the map. Compare the different maps and have the children talk about what they notice and what they think about the different ways that the maps were drawn or created.

Then go back to the McArthur map and talk about the language used to describe the map: upside down, not normal, wrong. Here you can talk to them about how language works in powerful ways that shape what we come to believe. Is the map really upside down or the wrong way? Could it be that some people see it in this way because they have not experienced a map any other way? Because of where the live in the world? Because of who first started creating maps?

References

McArthur's Universal Corrective Map. Retrieved January 10, 2012 from http:// odtmaps.com/detail.asp_Q_product_id_E_McA-23x35 Stuart McArthur's Universal Corrective Map. Retrieved January10, 2012, from http://www.youtube.com/ watch?v=QYuV4eOVz38

Chapter 6

The Tomato Trials

In a co-op class just outside Washington, DC, a small group of children wanted to plant tomatoes. In this cooperative class setting, parents work with the children on various school projects during the school day. The ratio was usually two adults to eight children. Planting has long been an activity of early childhood classrooms, whether this be planting flowers, plants, fruits, or vegetables. What differentiates the work we describe in this chapter is the use of technology not only as a tool for information gathering but as a tool for engaging in the analysis of those informational texts in terms of how such texts work to position the consumer in particular ways. The Tomato Trials project was led by Vivian and her son TJ, who at the time was six years old and at the end of kindergarten. They began with a conversation regarding where they could go to find the information they need to learn how to plant tomatoes.

Vivian

> We looked at books, we talked to people we knew had planted tomatoes in the past, and did an online search of ways to plant tomatoes. Our search revealed a number of possibilities many of which we had never heard of including the use of a tomato cage; a metal structure that tomato plants cling to for support as they grow.

The following three possibilities were of greatest interest to the group:

1. Planting tomatoes from seed—planting tomato seeds directly into planting pots.
2. Transplanting small tomato plants—buying small tomato plants and transplanting them into larger planting pots.
3. Using the Topsy Turvey Tomato Planter—a method of growing tomatoes upside down using a plastic bag.

They then realized how many different kinds of tomatoes they could grow, so the next step was to do some research on what kind of tomato would grow best in the area where they would be doing their planting.

Backbreaking Work?

While searching for possible ways to plant tomatoes, however, an advertisement for the Topsy Turvey Tomato planter caught TJ's attention. In particular, he wondered about the use of the phrase *back-breaking work*, asking what it means and "whose back are [the advertisers] talking about?"

Vivian

We decided to start by looking more closely at the commercial. Although we first saw it as a television ad, we were able to find it on YouTube. This gave us the benefit of being able to pause the video so that we could take a closer look at certain images. For instance parts of the commercial are in color and parts are in black and white.

We noticed the black and white portions of the commercial were used when talking about the "back breaking work," which was being done by a man. The image clearly showed a man in physical pain from having to bend down and plant tomatoes in the ground. In fact, the children engaged in reenactments of this scene in the ad.

The commercial then switched to color when the Topsy Turvey Tomato Planter was brought into the picture. This time a woman, with a smile on her face, looked as though she was effortlessly planting tomatoes using the Planter.

"That doesn't seem fair. Anyone can actually use it. Like Jim used a Topsy Turvey also."

With his comment, TJ was referring to how the ad worked to position men as the ones who can do backbreaking work. Subsequently, the unspoken message is that women cannot do this work. Similarly, the ad works to position women as the people for whom the Topsy Turvey Planter would be most appropriate, thereby simultaneously working to position a man who might use this planter as not able to do "manly" back breaking work. TJ counters this by relating to someone he knows, who is a man named Jim and uses the planter for his tomato planting. His comment, "that doesn't seem fair" refers to the way in which the ad implies that only men and not women can do backbreaking work.

Critically Reading the Web

Baildon and Damico (2011), in their book *Social Studies as New Literacies in a Global Society: Relational Cosmopolatinism in the Classroom,* note, "At the end of the first decade of the 21st century, there is no shortage of scholars striving to better understand the substance and impact of the ways new technology tools are transforming our thinking, interactions, and lives" (p. 53). They ask how Web-based inquiry tools and resources might be used to support teachers and students to engage in Web-based inquiry. They then describe the Critical Web Reader,

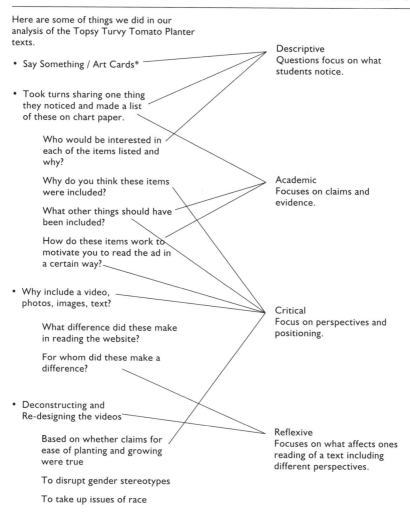

Here are some of things we did in our analysis of the Topsy Turvy Tomato Planter texts.

• Say Something / Art Cards*

• Took turns sharing one thing they noticed and made a list of these on chart paper.

Who would be interested in each of the items listed and why?

Why do you think these items were included?

What other things should have been included?

How do these items work to motivate you to read the ad in a certain way?

• Why include a video, photos, images, text?

What difference did these make in reading the website?

For whom did these make a difference?

• Deconstructing and Re-designing the videos

Based on whether claims for ease of planting and growing were true

To disrupt gender stereotypes

To take up issues of race

Descriptive
Questions focus on what students notice.

Academic
Focuses on claims and evidence.

Critical
Focus on perspectives and positioning.

Reflexive
Focuses on what affects ones reading of a text including different perspectives.

Figure 6.1 Critically Reading Topsy Turvy Chart

an online tool they created for guided inquiry into texts on the World Wide Web. Primarily created for use with older children, the Critical Web Reader tool requires students to enter text in response to questions about particular online texts. Each of these is framed using particular lenses: descriptive, academic, critical, and reflexive. For instance, through a critical lens, students might respond to a question such as, "What techniques does the author/creator use to influence me; loaded words, use of images, use of links, other" (2011, p. 68). Vivian used these lenses to reflect on what had been done in terms of analyzing the Planter ad as a way of thinking about how tools such as the Critical Web Reader might be of use to younger students. The chart in Figure 6.1 summarizes this reflection and shows intersections between the lenses.

Vivian

Aside from analyzing text and images from the ad, we also used Tagxedo, a Web-based program available for free that can be used to create word clouds. We created word clouds using the Web site addresses of different sites dealing with planting tomatoes, including the Topsy Turvey Tomato Planter site.

REFECTION POINT 6.1

Vivian

Although we acted out various new scenarios for the commercial, creating new dialogue, we didn't take it any farther than to role-play for ourselves as a way to redesign the ads. It would have been wonderful to have the children create a new "script" for the commercial, act it out, record it, and then post it on Youtube or another space to make the reconstructions available and useful to a broader audience.

For those worried about maintaining the children's anonymity, this could always be done using puppets or as voice only accompanied by drawn images such as a VoiceThread like the ones created by the children in Chapter 2.

How might you use technology to redesign or reconstruct the commercial to disrupt the gender stereotype or other social issue at play?

Another similar piece of software, Wordle, does the same kind of thing. A version of it is also available online for free. On the Wordle site, a word cloud is described as clouds or clusters of words that "… give greater prominence to words that appear more frequently in the source text." (January 28,2012 http://www.wordle.net/) With either Tagxedo or Wordle, you are asked to enter text from a document or Web page or the Web page url address that is then turned into a word cloud. The advantage of using Tagxedo is that a word cloud can be created in the shape of whatever objects you want. Figure 6.2 consists of two word clouds in the shape of tomatoes—word tomatoes—that Vivian and TJ created to analyze and compare two Web sites: The Vegetable Garden and The Topsy Turvey Tomato Planter. Figure 6.3 and Figure 6.4 are the charts that were created while reviewing the data provided through the word *tomatoes*.

Vegetable Garden website
http://www.vegetable-garden-guide.com/how-to-grow-tomatoes.html

Topsy Turvy website
https://www.topsyturvy.com

Figure 6.2 Word Tomatoes

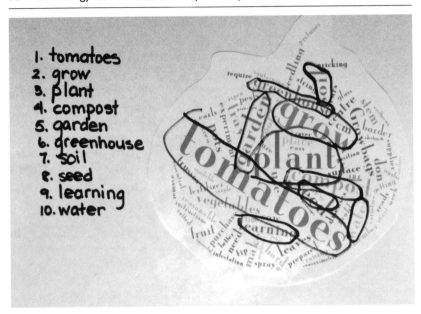

1. tomatoes
2. grow
3. plant
4. compost
5. garden
6. greenhouse
7. soil
8. seed
9. learning
10. water

Figure 6.3 Vegetable Garden Analysis

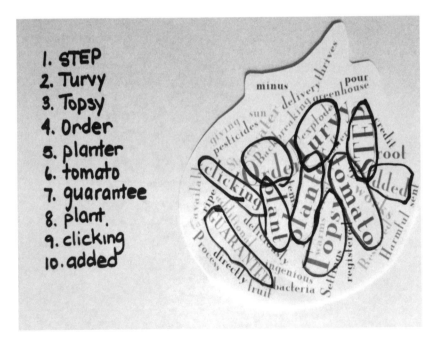

1. STEP
2. Turvy
3. Topsy
4. Order
5. planter
6. tomato
7. guarantee
8. plant
9. clicking
10. added

Figure 6.4 Topsy Turvy Analysis

Vivian

The first thing that we did with each word tomato is to highlight ten words that stood out. I arbitrarily chose the number ten because I thought it would give us enough words to work with but yet keep it manageable. We highlighted the words by circling them on the image. We then took those words and arranged them in order of size and then talked about why certain words such as "tomatoes" might have appeared in large font. We then talked about whether we could predict whether this site was a good site for learning to plant tomatoes.

When we looked at the word *tomato* for the Vegetable Garden site, the consensus was that "All the important things about planting tomatoes are big" and "this site has tomatoes, grow, plant, garden...all the things we need to know about for planting" (see Figure 6.3).

When we looked at the word *tomato* for the Topsy Turvy site, however, the words that were highlighted were very different. The comment, "This one is just about ordering the Topsy Turvy" pretty well sums up the responses to whether this site was a good one to teach us about planting tomatoes. No wonder, as the top four dominant words were STEP, Turvy, Topsy and Order (see Figure 6.4).

The Trials Begin

As a result to of this analysis of the Topsy Turvy Planter ad, the Tomato Trials were born as a science experiment whereby the growth of the tomatoes using each of the three options would be recorded over a period of time (see Figure 6.5 Tomato Trials) and the claims made by the Topsy Turvy company would be reviewed.

Tomato Trial Findings

Vivian

After planting three ways, we went back to the claims made in the Topsy Turvy (TT) ad. In particular, we thought about how "backbreaking" the planting was and decided there was actually nothing backbreaking about our experience. Planting in pots called for the same amount of work as using the TT. The challenge with the TT, however, was that we had to find a way to secure the planter so that it could hang off the ground. We decided that maybe if we had a lot to plant, we would have had more difficulty. Perhaps in that case planting seeds might have required less effort than replanting or using the TT. Given our planting experience, TJ further concluded, "boys or girls could plant any of these ways!"

In terms of the growth rate of the plants, after one week the potted transplant grew one-and-a-half inches more than the TT plant. However, after two weeks,

---

Resource Box 6.1

 Word Clouds

- Tagxedo
  http://www.tagxedo.com/
- Wordl
  http://www.wordle.net/

Possible Uses for Word Clouds

1. Analysis
   As word clouds create images that correspond to the frequency with which words appear, you could create word clouds to compare what is highlighted in various texts or websites. You could also then compare and contrast the words in terms of how they work to position a consumer of that text. What kinds of words appear most frequently? What kinds of words don't appear that you may have expected to see? What kind of effects do the words that appear most frequently have on you as a consumer? For instance, words such as "guaranteed," "safe," or "free" cause different reactions/actions from viewers of a text.

2. Editing
   Word clouds can be used to provide a quick overview of the kinds of words that are used or overused in a particular text.

3. Promoting or Advertising
   You could create a word cloud to promote what a particular text might be about. For instance, you could create a word cloud poster that speaks to the kinds of topics and issues you take up in your classroom by using text from a selection of books that you use with your students.

4. Art
   Word clouds could be used as art pieces. With Tagxedo, for instance, you can create word clouds overlaid on photographs or word clouds in various shapes and colors.

---

the TT plant had grown four inches taller than the potted transplant. Hannah thought that, "maybe it's gravity."

By the time the potted and TT plants started to bear fruit, which happened at the same time, they were about the same size. The seeded plant, however,

Figure 6.5 Tomato Trials

was still only two-and-a-half inches tall. Not too long after the first harvest, however, the area experienced a lot of rain. The potted plant and seeded plant survived the storm, but the soil in the TT planter absorbed so much water that the entire container fell to the ground, snapping the plant in two. This was disappointing, to say the least, as the plant had several pieces of fruit that did not get a chance to ripen. After some discussion, TJ suggested that perhaps "the ad could have talked about what happens when it rains instead of doing all that video about backbreaking work!" We then talked some more about why that might be the kind of information advertisers would not want to include in their ads. We talked about who would be interested in that kind of information and why. We also then talked about what we might add to the commercial. "Maybe just say hang it where it gets sun but not rain," was one suggestion. Another was "Make sure you hang it really good so it doesn't fall down in case the soil is too soaked." Yet another suggestion was not to revise the commercial at all but rather come up with a different product because the current one did not live up to its promise.

In the end, what started out as inquiry into how to plant tomatoes turned into a bigger cross-curricular event. The Topsy Turvy Tomato Trials created a space for:

- deconstructing and critically analyzing an everyday text;
- imagining how things could be otherwise;
- taking up issues of gender equity;
- exploring how ads work to position consumers;
- redesigning a public text;
- engaging in cross-curricular work (math, science, language arts, social studies); and
- taking on the roles of researcher and analyst.

Try This 6.1

Word Clouds as One Tool for Analysis with Young Children

Have a look at the word cloud in Figure 6.6. Cutting and pasting all the text from this book into Wordle created it. What does the word cloud tell you about the book?

Try creating a Tagxedo or Wordle cloud with your students using short stories or words from a Web site that is of interest to the children and have them Say Something* (Short, Harste, with Burke, 1996) about what they learn from the words and the size of the words that appear in the cloud.

*Say Something is a strategy whereby rather than following up a story or any sort of experience with a text by asking questions, you simply ask the children to share what is on their minds, to say something!

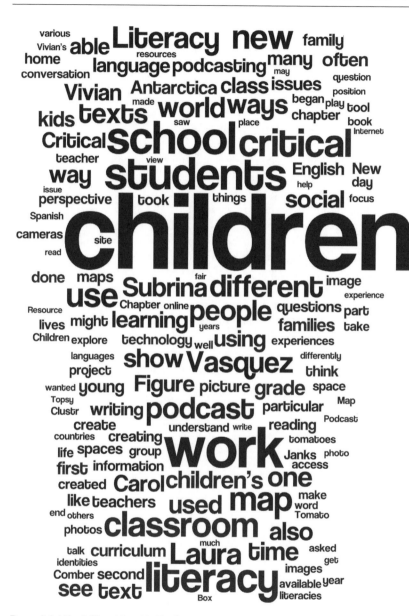

Figure 6.6 Word Cloud for this Book

In Retrospect

Shashi Bellamkonda, *social media expert extraordinaire* in the Washington, DC area and one of Vivian's Facebook friends, recently posted,

> My son was very insistent I share this video with my friends in Social Media. Yes he used the words "Social Media" … This is definitely the kind of conversation that takes place in my house.

The video to which Shashi is referring is one of his six-year-old son playing with a Fisher Price Cars play set. Apparently after recording his play, he insisted that his father share the video. Shashi then uploaded it to YouTube and then posted about it on Facebook. His comment, "This is definitely the kind of conversation that takes place in my house," signifies that his son was likely born into a home where new information communication technologies are part of the everyday. His son's request for the video to be shared with his friends in social media implies an understanding that social media is about friends. It also implies that at a young age, he is clearly aware that social media sites are places where information is shared and made accessible to a broader audience.

If only Shashi's son had been part of the Topsy Turvy Tomato Trials, he would probably have asked to post the video of the work to a social media space and that would definitely have brought a more critical edge to the work.

In the next chapter, we enter the classroom of Laura Herring and her second grades students as they hit the ground clicking into the world of photography.

Chapter 7

Picture This
Using Photography as a Tool for Critical Literacy

Jasmine: People see things in different ways. You can't expect people to see things the way you do.

Sita: If everyone saw stuff in the same ways, it wouldn't be interesting. Perspectives kind of matter.

Emma: Perspectives and opinions are linked.

In this chapter, we enter the second grade classroom where Laura Herring teaches a group of twenty-six children between the ages of six and eight years with a co-teacher. The private school is located in Washington, DC, in a middle-class neighborhood.

The opening exchange took place as Laura and the children engaged in a conversation about "perspective." This conversation comes from her attempts to create spaces for critical literacy in her classroom. Talking about perspective was part of their discussion on identity and positioning; constructs that serve as tools for understanding:

- that texts are socially constructed from particular points of view;
- that all texts are mediated through discourses (ways of being, doing, thinking, acting…); and
- that we can never speak outside of discourse.

These are also constructs for considering the positionings and perspectives we bring to our readings of texts; what Scollon and Scollon (2004) refer to as the historical bodies through which we participate as actors in life. The children were soon to begin a photography project for which these constructs were central concerns.

We met Laura while she was a graduate student working on a master's degree in curriculum and instruction at American University, where she took courses with each of us. Since that time, we have become colleagues and friends. What drew us to Laura was her deep interest in critical literacy and her commitment to create spaces for it not only in her own classroom but in her school, with her colleagues.

In a reflection crafted for one of the courses she took with us, she wrote,

> Settling into my seat, waiting for Vivian Vasquez's Topics in Literacy class at American University to begin, I noticed a black and white photograph sitting on the table in front of a classmate. I was immediately taken by this image. It was a close-up of a young African American boy eating a juicy peach Through his wide grin, he took a bite out of this delicious fruit. I could feel his delight as he tasted the sweetness. The moment was captured by the close-up stance of the photographer who took the picture at the child's eye-level. The black and white film added a certain mystique to the image, leaving me to imagine the colors that could have filled in the spaces of that instant. I was transfixed.
>
> I immediately inquired as to the origin of this photo. My classmate told me about Wendy Ewald's Literacy Through Photography program in which the Washington, DC public school she taught at was currently participating. The photographer of this image (and all the others she proceeded to show me) was a first grade child. I was floored. In my personal life, I love to take pictures, considering different angles, what to zoom in on and what to leave out, though I am by no means an expert. Looking at the picture again and considering the photographer was a seven-year-old brought my amazement to a whole new level. I was seeing the world through her eyes. I was seeing what she saw and how she saw it and I was spellbound.

I Wanna Take Me A Picture

The very next day, Laura ordered a copy of Wendy Ewald's (2002) book, *I Wanna Take Me a Picture*. In her book, Ewald details how photography can be used as a vehicle for self-expression, noting that taking pictures and writing about them are ways to bring students' lives into the classroom in a meaningful way. Excited about possible learning opportunities for her students, Laura immediately began adapting Ewald's ideas for use with her students. According to the author of the Literacy Through Photography Blog located at http://literacythroughphotography.wordpress.com/wendy-ewald/, Ewald has "...for thirty eight years collaborated in art projects with children, families, women, and teachers in Labrador, Colombia, India, South Africa, Saudi Arabia, Holland, Mexico, and the United States." In her biographical sketch, she notes her "...projects probe questions of identity and cultural differences" and that "in her work with children she encourages them to use cameras to record themselves, their families, and their communities, and to articulate their fantasies and dreams" (Ewald & Lightfoot, 2002).

Laura

When considering how to bring this project to life, I was driven by the idea of creating a "third space" as Jackie Marsh discusses in "Popular Culture, New Media and Digital Literacy in Early Childhood." Marsh (2005) writes, …students who are able, when teachers allow, to transform their identities within classroom contexts can create a 'third space' (Gutierrez, Baquedano-Lopez and Turner, 1997) in which schooled norms and student lived experience can meet and ensure that children have agency and voice (p. 30).

The notion of students' identities outside of school uniting in a meaningful way with their in-school identities carried this project forward in my mind. A second focus was to understand others' perspectives. By bringing your life into the classroom and learning about your peers' lives, students and teachers alike can begin to see and understand the world as others do. My co-teacher, Sharyn Miller, and I devised our plan or "unit" and we got to work.

Reflection, Summer 2011

Reading Images

Laura began by "reading images" with the kids. As an entire group, in small groups, or in partnerships, students looked at several different photographs from magazines, advertisements, newspapers, and Laura's own personal photo albums, or the Web (see Figure 7.1 and 7.2 Laura's Personal Photos)

Figure 7.1 Julia

Figure 7.2 Gramps

Laura

As an entry point to photography, I wanted the kids to think about why people take pictures. I used personal photos as examples of capturing moments, emotions, and memories. I chose to use pictures from my life, specifically of intimate family moments, as a way to share myself with the kids. Since I would soon be asking them to document pieces of their lives and share them with their classmates and teachers, I wanted to model what that might look like and sound like.

We started by zooming in on facial expressions. What can you learn about how the people in the pictures may be feeling by looking closely at their expressions? At body language? We widened our focus to include the setting.

The first image Laura shared was one of her lying down holding her baby niece, Julia, to her chest (see Figure 7.1). She asked the children, "Why do you think I'm lying on the couch with Julia? Do you think this picture was staged or spontaneous? What does it tell about my relationship with my new niece?"

Laura

After we wondered and shared ideas, I was able to give context. This was the first time I met Julia and she was my very first niece or nephew. I fell in love with her the instant I saw her and this photo represents a very sweet moment when she and I were lounging on the couch. We talked about interpretations may be right on or how, when people bring their own experiences to their thinking, there may be different ways of seeing the same image.

The second image Laura shared was that of her grandfather (see Figure 7.2).

Laura

I was very close to my grandfather, who died in 2008. The kids already knew about him, as I tend to tell stories and share memories regularly. This photo provided an example of a portrait that may have been more challenging to interpret. Without seeing the setting or having more context for the photo, the viewer is left to interpret the subject's face. We listed adjectives that could describe him, we wondered where he was, and how he was feeling in this moment. Since I am unsure of the circumstances of this photo, we had no "right" answer or conclusion. Analyzing this photo allowed us to use our observation and conversation skills to provide interpretation, coming back to the idea that we all bring our own experiences to our thinking, which leads us to create our own theories. At the end of this discussion, I told the kids that this photo is special to me because it is a close-up on Gramps' face and it helps me remember how gentle and kind he was. This frozen, captured moment elicits emotion within me, as seeing the image automatically allows me to hear his voice and remember our many good times together.

With each picture, they used the following questions to shape their discussion:

- What is the photographer's message?
- What can I learn from this photograph?
- Where was the photographer standing/sitting/etc. when he or she took this picture?

While reading the images, Laura had her students divide the photograph into four quadrants as a way to zoom in and look more intensely on each part of the image and, thereby, unpack its complexity. By concentrating on a particular part of the photograph, Laura observed that the children began noticing things they had not before.

Perspective and Positioning

This work led to interesting discussions about perspective and positioning. Laura used the book *Duck! Rabbit!* by Amy Krouse Rosenthal (2009) to explore the idea further. In the book, two unseen characters debate the identity or identities of the character or creature central to the book. The argument is whether this creature is a rabbit or a duck and is a clever take on the age-old optical illusion. Of course, the creature could be either: It all depends on the perspective and position from which you view the image(s). Laura connected this notion to reading photographs with her students;

Laura

The same is true with photographs; one may interpret them a certain way, while another sees something completely different. We bring our own experiences and identities to what we see and how we see it.

This led to a conversation among her students about perspective.

Laura reflected,

I was quite impressed by the kids' thinking. After several days of "reading images," the kids started to make plans for their own photographs in their writer's notebooks.

In conversation with Vivian, Laura decided to assign the following topics for the children to photograph:

- 5 self-portraits
- 5 family images
- 5 images representing "culture" 1 photograph of a tree
- 1 photograph representing the meaning of "fair" the remaining photos of any subject, topic, or issue of their choice.

Laura

As I walked around and conferenced with the kids, I consistently asked,

- What is your message?
- What do you want to communicate about yourself, your family, your culture?
- How will you do that? [communicate ideas]
- Where will the camera be?

Try This 7.1

Analyzing Photographs

One of the things Laura had her students do to help them to look more closely at the details and nuances of a photograph was to have them divide the photograph into four sections. This is a terrific way for them to better unpack images.

A great way to introduce children to this activity is to give them a sheet of dark-colored paper that has had one quarter cut out of it. They would then rotate the paper, positioning the cut-out portion over the section of the image upon which they would like to focus.

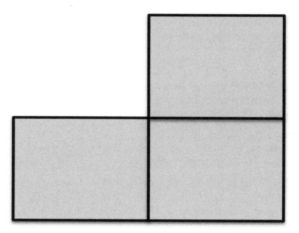

These probing questions helped the kids visualize their photographs.

Excitement had been building since the project was first introduced. It was no surprise that the children pretty well hit the ground clicking when the cameras were finally distributed. The cameras the children were given were Kodak disposables with black and white film.

Laura

I chose to use disposable cameras for two main reasons: access and patience. My school did not have enough digital cameras to provide one for each child in my class. It is likely that most families had one at home, but that was not a sure thing. Even if they did, the quality of the cameras could have varied and I wanted each child to have the same tools for the project. Considering these students were born in 2001 or 2002, their experience with film cameras was limited to none. Most of my second graders had never taken a roll of film to be developed, unsure of what the results would be, having to wait at least an hour to see the finished products. I thought using disposable cameras would provide an exercise in patience. There would be no immediate gratification of instantly seeing the image and having the option to delete or edit. The focus of this project was to capture moments, explore identity, and communicate messages. Worrying about getting it "perfect," I felt, would interfere with that work.

After a search online, Laura found the cameras being sold at a discounted rate at a wholesale Web site. She reflected,

> The kids were beside themselves with anticipation. The excitement had been building since the project was announced, and the day the cameras finally went home was a thrill for both the students and teachers.

After some tips on how to use the camera such as holding down the button to activate the flash and not blocking the viewing window with your finger, the cameras were taken home, and the photographers' work began.

Laura noted,

> It was interesting to see these 7 and 8-year olds navigate a disposable camera. Being born in 2003 or 2004, many had never used one before. They were used to digital camera or smart phones when you can see the image immediately, delete it, or edit it to your liking. With disposable cameras using actual 35-mm film, there would be no results until the film was dropped off at a camera store and developed the old fashioned way. This added an element of patience to the project.

The budding photographers had one full week to take all of their photos. Students were responsible for maintaining a photo log to record their shots. Laura had hoped that having to fill in the photo log after each shot would force the children to pause, reflect, and think before snapping their next photo. For each shot, a brief description was recorded, including a notation on whether the photograph was staged or candid.

The first camera was returned on day two while others trickled in throughout the week. There were also a couple of children who asked for an extra day of photographing. Julia, for example, was one person who requested an extension. In fact, her mother commented that Julia really took the picture-taking very seriously and that she planned each photo she took and was truly invested in the work. Her mother asked, "Could we have one more day so she can finish?" Laura was thrilled and readily agreed to give Julia more time.

In her reflection Laura wrote,

Once all of the cameras were turned in, I took them to a local camera shop to be developed. Surprised to see so many disposable cameras, the clerk automatically assumed they were from a wedding reception. "Nope, these are from my second grade students," I proudly explained.

The vibe in our classroom the day the photos were handed out rivaled the energy level the day the cameras went home. The anticipation had built to a crescendo and I could not wait to let the kids explore their work.

After rallying everyone together on the rug and explaining that the pictures were back, Laura described the children as "bouncing up and down with excitement."

Raj: I can't wait to see them!
Maggie: I hope the one of me in my cowgirl boots came out.

Laura gave each child an envelope of her or his pictures and told them to find a quiet space in the classroom to view them. Laura walked around the room, which was now buzzing with excitement, and sat with the kids as they explored:

Amy: This did not come out the way I thought.
Mary: I love this picture!
Hugh: One of my favorites came out!

Immediately there were opportunities to talk about perspective and positioning. From behind the viewfinder, Amy had expected to take a particular shot. However, once the image was put into print, the results were not as she had expected. What are possible reasons for this? Others were totally thrilled to see how their photos turned out.

Laura pulled up a chair next to Michael and listened as he shuffled through each picture:

Michael: Here's a picture of the football team my grandpa was on. There's my toothbrush! I used to play the djembe. My mom painted this picture right here. My dad playing piano! Here's another picture my mom painted. The Estonian flag. Here's my cat. I also have a dog, too. Here's Estonian clothes. Here's the Sri Lankan flag—my dad is from Sri Lanka. My grandpa's actually not too healthy. He has really bad cancer. Here's my mom talking to my dad. Here's Crayola—me and Reeves [his brother] love to be artistic. Here's my picture of fair. There's 5 action figures on each side.

Laura could barely get a word in edgewise as Michael brimmed with enthusiasm and pride. He could not wait to get to the next picture to explain what part of his life it represented. Sita felt the same way. She flipped through her photos with a similar energy and offered commentary for each one:

Sita: This is my friend. She comes over and we play soccer together. I accidentally took a picture of my butt. It was very inappropriate. This is my snow globe collection. The one in the middle I wanted to focus on because my grandmother gave it to me. She lives in Philadelphia. This is a picture of my messy desk. This is the Harry Potter book I'm reading with my mom. This is my guitar. These are my sister's shoes. The reason I took that picture is because whenever my family is going out somewhere, my mom screams at me because I refuse to wear dresses, the closest I get is a jean dress. My family is very fancy. This picture is because I'm a quarter Spaniard. I took a picture of a pig because I really like drawing. This is my Spanish class. My sister usually makes us have a dance party and here we are dancing.

For Michael and Sita, taking photographs created a space for their worlds to become more visible (Pahl and Rowsell, 2010). Through this activity, their voices were heard in ways they had not been before.

Drew, a student whom Laura described as "struggling mightily with academics," was often a challenge to engage. He is often resistant to try anything that is hard for him and is acutely aware of his abilities in relation to his peers. With diagnosed learning challenges, he receives outside support and is frequently frustrated in the classroom. After looking through his photos, he quietly tapped Laura on the shoulder and asked, "Can we do more of this?" Perhaps his resistance in the past was his way of voicing his feelings (Schultz, 2009). Is it possible that photography might be a way for Drew to voice his feelings and thinking differently?

Images and Words Come Together

After spending time with their photographs, Laura had the children write poetry about their photos. While exploring photography, Laura also had her students working on a poetry unit. As such, the children had spent a couple weeks reading different kinds of poetry and writing some of their own. Laura explained that once their photos were developed, they would be using what they had learned about poetry to write poems using the photos. The day the photos were distributed to the class, the excitement was palpable. After looking at each image and sharing with their peers, the children were eager to choose a favorite and to start writing. The photographs provided a powerful motivation to write (see Figures 7.3 and Figure 7.4). Laura's students were proud of their work and were thrilled to see parts of their home lives as part of the classroom.

She Still Will Keep Her Blanket

Ripped, torn, ragged
That's what she likes most.
Old, dirty, patched
That makes her heart dance
Twirled around as if by magic
That makes her blanket speak.
Over the city, over the dunes, over the world so wide
Traveling with her wherever she goes
Attached to her with a rope
As long as she lives, they will never let GO!

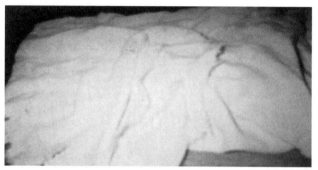

Figure 7.3 Blanket

A week or so after writing their poems, they were asked to choose the photo and poem they wanted displayed at the annual second grade assembly. Laura's plan was to scan, enlarge, and mount the photos and poems on stock paper for display (see Figure 7.3 and Figure 7.4) The event was an entire school assembly attended by the children's families. At the assembly, some of Laura's students explained the process pertaining to the photography project. The photographer poets were then asked to stand by their work, which was dispersed throughout the gym. Guests were then invited to view the images and poems close up. The second graders read their poems and answered any questions.

Laura: The audience is authentic and the kids take incredible pride in their work. The assembly was incredible. Again, the classroom was alive with excitement. So much had gone into this: learning to read images, thinking about what to communicate to the audience and how to do it, taking pictures and recording them in your log, writing poems and then choosing one in particular to revise, edit, and publish for an audience of hundreds.

Trees

Whoosh, whoosh!
Trees swaying in
The wind.
Whack, thwack!
Branches whacking in
The sky.
Tap, tap!
A beautiful bird taps
The trunk.
Whoosh, Thwack, Whack
Everything sounding
At the same time.
How many sounds?

Figure 7.4 Trees

After the assembly, the school's curriculum coordinator sent Laura and her teaching partner an e-mail:

Good morning Sharyn and Laura,

Your students brought tears to my eyes. Seriously, their personal investment in their poems and their photos were really touching. Also evident was how many different poetry-writing techniques they used in their work. From talking with Drew, I understood that some people revised extensively to distill their lengthier pieces down to the most interesting parts. From the group introduction to the individual displays, from the pets to the snow globes, and from the quiet readers to the dramatic ones, this unit clearly reached all your students and those of us fortunate to get a peek into their work today, what a huge success!

Laura reflected on the experience:

> After receiving such positive feedback from the students, their parents, and my colleagues, it was tempting to sit back and rest on my laurels for a bit to enjoy a job well done. The assembly was a success; we'd display the photos and poems in the hallway for a few weeks and then send them home with the kids.
>
> Now it's time to move on to the next unit. It's amazing how fast-paced teaching is. I often struggle to find the time to reflect upon the work we do, as there's always something else coming up. The objective of this work, however, was not simply to display poems and photos for all to see. It was to bridge home and school life, giving value to kids' multiple identities and to investigate the notion of perspective.
>
> Our conversation on perspective was impressive. The kids grabbed on to the idea that our experiences inform our perspectives. Seeing life through others' eyes, considering the lives our friends live helps us to understand and connect with others.

REFLECTION POINT 7.1

In one of Laura's reflections she wrote:

> Kids are often asked to write or draw about home ("Draw the place in your home where you do your best reading or write a personal narrative detailing an important experience you've had.") These are valuable practices and absolutely serve a similar purpose. What we found with the cameras, however, was that bringing these moments, people, and places into our classroom as captured images provided indisputable fodder for [powerful] conversations.

How might you make use of photography in your classroom?

The Power of the Photograph

While working on the photography project, Laura spoke of several surprises including the incredible sense of pride that the children displayed when sharing their work. Another surprise that caught her off guard involved a student who was not in her class.

Resource Box 7.1

  Resources on Wendy Ewald

- Literacy Through Photography Blog
  http://literacythroughphotography.wordpress.com/wendy-ewald/
- Portrait of a Photographer
  http://www.pbs.org/newshour/bb/entertainment/jan-june02/ewald/
- *Secret Games: Collaborative Works with Children, 1969–1999.* Scalo in association with Addison Gallery of American Art, Center for Documentary Studies, and Fotomuseum Winterthur, 2000.
- *I Dreamed I Had a Girl in My Pocket: The Story of an Indian Village.* New York, Center for Documentary Studies and W.W. Norton, 1996.
- *Magic Eyes: Scenes from an Andean Girlhood.* Seattle, WA: Bay Press, 1992.
- *I Wanna Take Me a Picture: Teaching Photography and Writing to Children.* Wendy Ewald and Alexandra Lightfoot. Boston, MA: Beacon Press, 2002.
- *The Best Part of Me: Children Talk About their Bodies in Pictures and Words.* Wendy Ewald. Boston, MA: Little, Brown Books for Young Readers, 2002.
- *Literacy and Justice Through Photography: A Classroom Guide (Language and Literacy Series).* Wendy Ewald, Katherine Hyde, and Lisa Lord. New York, NY: Teachers College Press, 2011.

Laura

Corey, in my class, chose to display a picture he took of his older sister, Carrie, at our assembly. His accompanying poem was about how great she is and how she is always willing to help him with his homework and play with him at home. Their family moved to DC from Texas at the beginning of the year, so they were both new to our school. Though I didn't know this, Carrie had been having somewhat of a hard time integrating with her peers.

At the school-wide assembly, I noticed a crowd of 6th grade students by Corey's display. I didn't think much of it. Some other 2nd graders had chosen photographs of their siblings and they tended to draw attention, as other kids knew them. The day after our assembly, one of the 6th grade teachers pulled me aside. He said some of his students were impressed by the fact that Carrie's little brother took a picture of her and wrote a poem about how wonderful she is as a big sister. He said immediately following the assembly, he overheard a 6th grader saying, "That's nice to write about her (Carrie)." I can't say that suddenly Carrie was surrounded by a new group of friends, but her teacher made it clear that some kids in the class started thinking differently about her and seemed more willing to give her a chance.

This was an unintended positive outcome of our work. Again, I think the power of the photograph was at play. A drawing or writing alone would have been easy to pass by. Seeing a concrete image of a person may lead to deeper thinking about who she is.

What is Fair?

In spite of her happiness with how the photography project played out, Laura wondered what she could have done to bring a more critical edge to the children's work. For instance, one of the assigned photographs was meant to focus on the meaning of fairness or being fair. We thought about this somewhat and thought that if fair is about everyone having a chance to participate and "voice" their passions, questions, and what is on their minds, it seems to us that although the children may not have photographed fairness, they did get a chance to live the experience of fairness. Through photography, the more vocal children described and talked about their photos and their lives in great detail. The quiet children may have let the photos do the talking for them, but their messages were heard just as loudly and just as powerfully, as when Ben shared his photo of his grandparents.

Laura

> … we could see his grandmother's gray hair and gentle smile. We saw the expression in her eyes and we were able to connect with her. We could think of our own grandparents and compare and contrast our families in tangible ways that may not be as available when reading descriptions or looking at illustrations.

In the end, Laura shared that even though she already had ideas for pushing the boundaries of the project, she continued to be proud of what her students had accomplished.

Laura

> I'm proud of the work my kids did. They rose to the challenge of negotiating their home and school identities in meaningful ways, they analyzed the concept of looking at things from different perspectives and practiced putting themselves in others' shoes. My second graders displayed their work

REFLECTION POINT 7.2

"New technologies" is used to refer to technological innovations that have been made possible through digitisation. It can include "old" technologies, such as radio and television, which have been transformed through the digital signal (Digital Beginnings).

Retrieved January 10, 2012,
from http://www.digitalbeginnings.shef.ac.uk/

Is a camera a new technology or an old technology? If we were to say that a non-digital camera is not a new technology, how might we do what Jackie Marsh at Digital Beginning suggests? Specifically, how do we transform it digitally?

in front of hundreds of people and explained their process with confidence. I look forward to planning more endeavors using technology to enhance my students' experiences.

In the next chapter, we share final thoughts regarding the potential and possibilities for working with children in early childhood settings at the intersection critical literacy and technology.

Try This 7.2

Word Image Posters

Have a look at the image below. It was created using a photograph that was scanned and then uploaded to Tagxedo (see Chapter 6). The text used to create the word image is Chapter 1 of this book. The image then could be used to make a statement about what we believe to be the focus of the book.

How might you use this strategy in your critical literacy work?

Chapter 8

Desires, Identities, and New Communication Technologies

Figure 8.1 A Preschool PowerPoint

Young children find themselves immersed in digital practices from an early age (Marsh et al., 2005; Thomas, 2011). As such, even when they do not have access to digital technologies at home, they often are still able to develop skills in working with digital texts and tools (Bearne et al., 2007). Take, for instance, the four children in Figure 8.1. They are part of a preschool classroom for four- and five-year-old children where their teacher asked them to do a presentation about a country of their choice. Vivian's son, TJ, wearing the baseball cap, was born into a family where PowerPoint is used for both work and play, so it is not surprising that he wanted to create a PowerPoint for his presentation on Canada. He did this together with his parents. In the photograph, he is talking about Niagara Falls and the Maid of the Mist boats, while his classmates listen intently. As they learn about Canada, they are simultaneously experiencing and becoming versed at what is possible with the use of a particular communicative tool. In conversation with TJ, they learn about what it means to put together a set of PowerPoint slides. Some of them grow in their curiosity and wish to be able to use PowerPoint themselves. Janks states, "[t]he desire for access to new ways of doing and being is what enables us to aspire to new identity positions" (2010: p. 222). Access without desire, however, does not result in creating spaces for new ways of being and doing. Similarly, to desire without access can lead to frustration. How then do we find ways of making accessible to our students the use of information communication technologies in meaningful ways that carry importance in their lives? At the same time that we value the importance of this question, we are also fully aware of the lack of resources for the purchase of hardware and software in some settings. We also realize that there is a need for teacher professional development in the use of technology. Keeping these issues in mind led us to deliberately include some demonstrations of practice using the kind of resources that are more readily available, such as cameras, television sets, and fax machines. In Chapter 3, for instance, where Kevan Miller's students worked to change the use of a problematic weather calendar, rather than using a networked television system, the children's performances could have been recorded using a video recorder and saved onto CDs or video tapes that could then be played in individual classrooms. Chapter 7 focuses on photography, which would require the use of a camera, which most schools now have for the use of teachers.

Meaningful and Sustained Learning

The children whom you read about in this book all engaged in sustained learning that they found meaningful in some way, whether that be creating a VoiceThread to raise funds for a school in Guatemala or finding ways to contribute to building sustainable communities. We would argue the principles of learning involved in the work done by these young children are similar to those Gee (2005) describes in his study of video gaming. For instance, Gee (2005) claims that "Learning a new domain…requires the learner to take on a new identity" (p. 34). What we saw throughout this book were demonstrations of the ways in which children readily played at being tech-savvy and performed identities such as podcaster or photographer. Gee further notes that "In a good game, words and deeds are all placed in the context of an interactive relationship between the player and the world" (p. 34). The children you read about sought out relationships as a way to communicate their passions, their desires, their frustrations, and their needs. For instance, the children Katie worked with used VoiceThreads to reach out to possible funders whereas Vivian's students sent out travel trunks across Canada containing postcards to be sent back so that they would know with whom they had made contact. The children were also producers of knowledge, risk takers as in Kristen's pre-K students, who explored the software they were using even before they were asked to do so. The children had agency as seen through their social action projects, and they often engaged in cross-functional work where they helped one another out on various tasks and taught one another what was needed to take on different roles, as Carol's second graders did while podcasting. All of these characteristics are included by Gee (2005) in his list of good learning principles.

Luke and Freebody (1999), in their study of the "roles" for the reader, identified different families of practices that individually are not sufficient but in combination are necessary: code breaker, text participant, text user, and critical text analyst. What they observed is that the most challenging of these roles and, therefore, the one least practiced in school settings is the role as critical text analyst (http://www.readingonline.org/research/lukefreebody.html). Comber notes that part of the problem is that we need more demonstrations of practice particularly in early childhood settings (2005). We hope this book contributes to that much-needed collection mentioned by Comber. We also hope that this book has created a space for you to think about what the technology that you do have available can afford the work that you do in your setting.

Learning from our Students

We probably would be well served to learn from two-year-old Lilina, who was at a playground with her mother when she decided to take a drive in a red and yellow ride-on car. As she opened the door to the car, she turned around facing her mother with her hand outstretched and said, "Keys." Her mother proceeded to hand her a set of toy keys, at which time Lilina began to enter the vehicle. Before entering the car completely, she turned toward her mother once more with her hand outstretched and said, "Phone." Her mother handed her a toy phone, and away she went. Lilina knows how to play technology even before she has access to it. Eight-year-old AJ does something similar as he writes "tweets," short statements used by those who use Twitter, a social networking tool, even though he does not have a Twitter account. Lilina and AJ, in the words of Wohlwend (2009, p. 136) are "early adopters." Wohlwend defines early adopters as signaling "two simultaneous identities for young technology users: (1) as developing learners of new literacies and technologies; and (2) as curious explorers who willingly play with new media" (p. 117).

Although on its own curiosity is not enough, the pleasure that comes with new discoveries and opportunities "can renew us" (Janks, 2010, p. 224) and could, therefore, be a great place to start to explore at the intersection of technology and critical literacy. Getting going is important for, as Luke (1999) reminds us, "as we are all being pushed onto the on-ramps of the information superhighway" (p. 99) that it is "crucial for educators at all levels of schooling to take charge of reshaping curriculum and pedagogy in relation to [technology]" (1999, p. 99).

The problem is "if we don't corporate software developers will [continue] to maintain their control over content design that invariably shapes how and what we teach" (Luke, p. 99).

Try This 8.1

Technology Day

One of the roadblocks to using technology in early childhood classrooms is the fear of the unknown. In particular, we have in mind parents or caregivers who have genuine concerns with allowing their child to use technological tools such as computers and tablets such as iPads. During her days as an early childhood teacher, one of the things that Vivian did to ease parental worries around computer use was to have a computer play day or technology fair where parents were invited to try out various computer programs and technological tools themselves. Often, it was the children who guided the adults through the various software and hardware.

Products created by children such as digital graphics and stories done using computer technology were shared along with projects that were created with the aid of research online. E-based Web sites such as the one we created for Carol's second graders' 100% Kids Podcast were also shared.

Teachers like those you read about in the previous chapters have begun to take charge and reshape curriculum with new technologies in mind. This, of course, is especially important given the state of affairs that we find ourselves in where, as noted on the Web site of the Early Childhood Education Assembly, "Mandates to implement practices that are antithetical to what we embrace as supportive of young children's literacy learning are pervasive" (retrieved January 10, 2012, from http://www.eceassembly.blogspot.com. Further, "Teachers of young children are asked to teach-to-the-test in ways that take away opportunities for holistic, thoughtful, play-oriented practices that allow children to construct knowledge through contextualized and purposeful experiences" (Early Childhood Education Assembly, 2007).

Carrington (2008) asserts,

> For literacy education to make a real difference in the lives and futures of the young people who move in and out of complex social fields and who are growing up in a post-traditional risk society, it is necessary to acknowledge that childhood is not what it used to be and that curricula, school hierarchies and classrooms cannot, therefore, continue to be what they used to be (p. 164).

Speaking of not continuing what they used to be, in the photograph of TJ's classroom in Figure 8.1, it is interesting to note that a PowerPoint presentation is unfolding between a job chart and a growth chart—both longstanding artifacts associated with early-years classrooms. Perhaps this sort of 'third space' where home literacies and school literacies come together could be the kind of space that some of us might need to imagine curriculum anew. What might you try in your setting?

Resource Box 8.1

 Online Tools

Name of Site	Url Address	Site Description
edublogs	http://edublogs.org/	Education blog hosting site
VoiceThread	http://voicethread.com/	Collaborative multi-media slide show
Wordle	http://www.wordle.net/	Tool for generating word clouds
Tagxedo	http://www.tagxedo.com/	Tool for creating shaped word clouds
Bitstrips for School	http://www.bitstripsfor schools.com/	Tool for creating comic strips
PhotoPeach	http://photopeach.com/	Online slides show
Kerpoof	http://www.kerpoof.com/	Creating art and movies or text with animation
WorldMapper	http://www.worldmapper.org/	Interactive Maps
Storybird	http://storybird.com/	Flip storybooks
Odosketch	http://sketch.odopod.com/	Sketching Tools

References

Baildon, M., & Damico, J. S. (2011). *Social studies as new literacies in a global society: Relational cosmopolitanism in the classroom*. New York: Routledge.

Bearne, E., Clark, C., Johson, A., Manford, P., Motteram, M., & Wolstencroft, H. (2007). *Reading on screen*. Liecester. UK: UKLA.

Bers, M. (2008). *Blocks to robots: Learning with technology in the early childhood classroom*. New York: Teachers College Press.

Bourdieu, P. (1977). *Outline of a theory of practice*. Cambridge, UK: Cambridge University Press.

Brougere, G. (2006). Toy houses: A socio-anthropological approach to analyzing objects. *Visual Communication,* 5(1):5–24.

Carrington, V. (2005). New textual landscapes, information, new childhood. In J. Marsh (Ed.), *Popular culture: Media and digital literacies in early childhood* (pp. 13–27). London, UK: Sage.

Carrington, V. (2008). I'm Dylan, I'm not going to say my last name: Some thoughts on childhood, text and new technologies. *British Educational Research Journal*, 32(2):151–166.

Comber, B. (2001). Negotiating critical literacies. *School Talk*, 6(3):1–2.

Comber, B. (2003). Critical literacy: What does it look like in the early years? In N. Hall, J. Larson, & J. Marsh (Eds.), *Handbook of research in early childhood literacy* (pp. 355–368). London, UK: Sage/Paul Chapman.

Comber, B. (Contributor). (2005). Critical literacy. In J. Larson & J. Marsh, *Making literacy real* (pp. 40–67). Thousand Oaks, CA: Sage.

Comber, B. (in press, 2012). Literacy for a sustainable world. In A. Simpson, *Language, literacy and literature*. Oxford University Press. (Accepted November, 2011).

Comber, B., Nixon, H., & Reid, J. (Eds.). (2007). *Literacies in place: Teaching environmental communications*. Newtown, NSW, Australia: Primary English Teachers Association.

Comber, B., & Simpson, A. (Eds.). (2001). *Critical literacy at elementary sites*. Mahwah, NJ: Lawrence Erlbaum Associates.

"Early Childhood Education Assembly." Retrieved from http://www.eceassembly. blogspot.com/

Evans, J. (Ed.)(2005). *Literacy moves on*. London: David Fulton Publishers

Ewald, W., & Lightfoot, A. (2002). *I wanna take me a picture: Teaching photography and writing to children*. Ypsilanti, MI: Beacon Press.

Ewald, W., Hyde, K., & Lord, L. (2011). *Literacy and justice through photography: A classroom guide* (Language and Literacy Series). New York: Teachers College Press.

Frank, B. (2008). Critical Literacies. Keynote presentation given at the InterLERN Summer Institute. Mississauga, Ontario, Canada. July 2008.

Freebody, P. & Luke, A. (1990). Literacies programs: Debates and demands in cultural context: Prospect. *Australian Journal of TESOL*, 5(7):7–16.

Freire, P., & Macedo, D. (1987). *Literacy: Reading the word and the world*. South Hadley, MA: Bergin & Garvey.

Gee, J. P. (1999). *An introduction to discourse analysis theory and method* (2nd ed.). New York: Routledge.

Gee, J. P. (2003). *What video games have to teach us about learning and literacy*. New York: Palgrave/Macmillan.

Gee, J. P. (2005). Good video games and good learning. *Phi Kappa Phi Forum*, 85(2):34–37.

Gutiérrez, K., Baquedano-López, P. & Turner, M.G. (1997). Putting language back into the language arts: When the radical middle meets the third space. *Language Arts*, 74(5), 368–378.

Hartmann, W., & Brougere, G. (2004). Toy culture in pre-school education and children's toy preferences. In Goldstein et al. (Eds.), *Toys, games, and media* (pp. 37–54). Sussex, UK: Psychology Press.

Janks, H. (1993). *Language, identity, and power*. Johannesburg, South Africa: Witwatersrand University Press.

Janks, J. (2010). *Literacy and power*. New York: Routledge.

Janks, H., & Comber, B. (2006). Critical literacy across continents. In K. Pahl, & J. Rowsell (Eds.). *Travel notes from the New Literacy Studies: Instances of practice* (pp. 226–248). Clevedon, UK: Multilingual Matters.

Janks, H., & Vasquez, V. (2011). Critical literacy revisited: Writing as critique. *English Teaching: Practice and Critique*, 10(1):1–6. Retrieved from http://edlinked.soe.waikato.ac.nz/research/journal/view.php?id=54&p=1

Kohn, A. (2007). *Re-thinking homework*. Principal. Alexandria, VA: NAESP.

Krouse Rosenthal, A. (2009). *Duck Rabbit*. San Francisco, CA: Chronicle Books.

Larson, J., & Marsh, J. (2005). *Making literacy real*. Thousand Oaks, CA: Sage.

Lankshear, C., & Knobel, M. (2007). *A new literacies sampler*. New York: Peter Lang.

Luke, C. (1999). What next? Toddler netizens, playstation thumb, techno-literacies, *Contemporary Issues in Early Childhood*, 1(1):95–100.

Luke, A. (2007). The body literate: Discourse and inscription in early literacy. In T. Van Dijk (Ed.), *Discourse studies (vol. IV, pp. 1–22)*. London, UK: Sage Publications.

Luke, A., & Freebody, P. (1999). Further notes on the four resources model. *Reading Online*, Retrieved from readingonline.org/research/lukefreebody.html

Manning, A. (1993). Curriculum as conversation. Keynote given at the *Western Australia Reading Conference*. May 22, 1993.

Marsh, J. (2002). Popular culture, computer games and the primary curriculum. In M. Monteith (Ed.), *Teaching primary literacy through ICT* (pp. 127–143) .Buckinghamshire, UK: Open University Press.

Marsh, J. (2005). (Ed). *Popular culture, new media and digital literacy in early childhood*. New York: Routledge Press.

Marsh, J., Brooks, P., Hughes, J., Ritchie, L., Roberts, S, & Wright, K. (2005). *Digital beginnings: Young people's use of popular culture, media and new technologies*. Sheffield, UK: University of Sheffield Research Center.

Meacham, S. J. (2003, March). Literacy and street credibility: Plantations, prisons, and African American literacy from Frederick Douglass to Fifty Cent. Presentation at the *Economic and Social Research Council Seminar Series Conference*, Sheffield, United Kingdom, March, 2003.

Mijak, J.L. (2010) "'Lost Boy of Sudan' announces school-building collaboration with Mothering Across Continents and Sudan Sunrise." Press release, November 5. Sudan Sunrise. http://www.sudansunrise.org/news/2010/5/lost-boy-sudan-announces-school-building-collaboration-mothering-across-continents-and (Retrieved February 1 2012).

Moll, L. C., Amanti, C., Neff, D., & Gonzalez, N. (1992). Funds of knowledge for teaching: Using a qualitative approach to connect homes and classrooms. *Theory into Practice*, 31(2):132–141.

Morgan, W. (1997). *Critical literacy in the classroom: The art of the possible.* New York: Routledge.

Nixon, A. S., & Gutierrez, K. D. (2008). Digital literacies for young English learners: Productive pathways toward equity and robust learning. In C. Genishi & A. L. Goodwin (Eds.), *Diversities in early childhood: Rethinking and doing* (pp. 121–135). New York: Routledge.

O'Brien, J. (2001). Children reading critically. A local history. In B. Comber & A. Simpson (Eds.), *Critical literacy at elementary sites* (pp. 37–54). Mahwah, NJ: Lawrence Erlbaum Associates.

Pahl, K., & Rowsell, J. (2010). *Artifactual literacies: Every object tells a story.* New York: Teachers College Press.

Reinl, J. (2011). South Sudan's 'lost boys' set to return home. *The National*, Retrieved from http://www.thenational.ae/news/world/africa/south-sudans-lost-boys-set-to-return-home.

Scollon, R., & Scollon, S. W. (2004). Nexus analysis: discourse and the emerging Internet. New York: Routledge.

Schultz, K. (2009). *Rethinking classroom participation: Listening to silent voices.* New York: Teachers College Press.

Short, K. G., Harste, J. C., with Burke, C. (1996). *Creating classrooms for authors and inquirers.* Portsmouth, NH: Heinemann.

Souto-Manning, M. (2012). Unpublished manuscript.

Souto-Manning, M., & Felderman, C. (2012). Negotiating critical literacies: Toward full inclusion in early childhood classrooms. In V. Vasquez & J. Wood. (Eds.), *Perspectives and provocations in early childhood education.* Charlotte, NC: Information Age Publishing.

Thomas, M. (Ed.). (2011). *Deconstructing digital natives.* New York: Routledge Press.

Uprichard, E. (2008). Children as 'being and becomings': Children, childhood and temporality. *Children & Society*, 22:303–313.

Vasquez, V. (1994). A step in the dance of critical literacy. *UKRA Reading*, 28(1):39–43.

Vasquez, V. (1998). Building equitable communities: Taking social action in a kindergarten classroom. *Talking Points*, 9(2):3–7

Vasquez, V. (1999). *Negotiating critical literacies with young children.* Unpublished doctoral dissertation, Indiana University, Bloomington.

Vasquez, V. (2001). Constructing a Critical Curriculum with Young Children. In Comber, B. & Simpson, A. (Eds.). *Critical Literacy at Elementary Sites* (pp. 55–66). Mahwah, NJ: Lawrence Erlbaum Associates.

Vasquez, V. (2004). *Negotiating critical literacies with young children.* New York: Routledge Press.

Vasquez, V. (2005). Creating spaces for critical literacy with young children: Using everyday issues and everyday text. In J. Evans (Ed.), *Literacy moves on* (pp. 78–97). Abingdon, UK: David Fulton Publishers.

Vasquez, V. (2010a). *Getting beyond "I like the book": Creating spaces for critical literacy in K-6 classrooms.* Newark, DE: International Reading Association.

Vasquez, V. (2010b). A podcast is born: Critical literacy and new technologies. In V. Vasquez (Ed.), *Getting beyond I like the book: creating spaces for critical literacy in K-6 Classrooms.* Newark, DE: International Reading Association.

Vasquez, V. (2010c). iPods, puppy dogs, and podcasts: Imagining literacy instruction for the 21st century. *School Talk,* 15(2):1–2.

Vasquez, V., & Egawa, K. (2003). *Critical literacy: Putting a critical edge on your teaching focused study.* Urbana, IL: National Council of Teachers of English.

Vasquez, V., & Harste, J.C. (2010). Kid-watching, negotiating, and podcasting: Imagining literacy instruction for the 21st century. In Association of Literacy Educators and Researchers (Eds.). Arlington, TX: Texas A&M University. *Yearbook,* (32):17–30.

Wohlwend, K. (2009). Early adopters: Playing literacies and pretending new technologies in print-centric classrooms. *Journal of Early Childhood Literacy.* 9(2):117–140.

Wohlwend, K. (2011). *Playing their way into literacies.* New York: Teachers College Press.

Wood, D., & Kaiser, W. L. (2001). *Seeing through maps: The power of images to shape our world view.* Amherst, MA: ODT.

Wu, T. (2010, March 22). Bandwidth is the new black gold. *TIME Magazine.* Retrieved December 19, 2011 from http://www.newamerica.net/node/29005

About the Authors

Vivian Vasquez

Vivian is a professor of education at American University (AU). Her research interests are in critical literacy, early literacy, and information communication technology. Prior to coming to AU, Dr. Vasquez taught preschool and public school for fourteen years. Since then, she has held appointive and elective offices in scholarly organizations including The National Council of Teachers of English, The American Educational Research Association, The International Reading Association, and The Whole Language Umbrella. Her awards include the James N. Britton Award (2005) and the AERA Division B Outstanding Book of the Year Award (2006). Both awards were for her book *Negotiating Critical Literacies with Young Children*. She was also the first recipient of the AERA Teacher Research SIG Dissertation Award (2004). Vivian is host of the CLIP (critical literacy in practice) Podcast located at www.clippodcast.com. More than anything, she is proudest to be TJ's mommy.

Carol Felderman

Carol taught second and third grade for seven years in Fairfax, VA. She went on to pursue her doctorate in education, specifically literacy studies in early childhood. Currently, she is part of the adjunct faculty at American University and continues to write about literacy experiences with young children. Recently, her family has grown with the birth of her daughter, Lily, who joins her son, Liam, husband, Jim, and two dogs, Miles and Maggie.

The authors thank the following individuals for generously sharing their stories with us and contributing them to this book.

Kristin Lupino

Kristen student taught at both Francis-Stevens Education Campus and Bright Beginnings during her graduate studies in early childhood education at American

University, which she completed in May 2011. She is now a preschool (three-year-old) teacher at Francis-Stevens, a DC public school, where she is continuing to ensure equal access to technology for all of her students.

Katie Stover

Katie recently completed her doctorate at University of North Carolina at Charlotte. She is a former elementary teacher and literacy coach. Her research interests include translating research and theory into classroom practice, critical literacy, writing instruction, and teacher education. *She has published in journals including The Reading Teacher and Middle School Journal.*

Laura Herring

Laura Herring has taught second and fourth grades in both public and independent school settings over the last nine years. Highly motivated by her recent graduate studies at American University, she is passionate about providing space for critical literacy work and identity exploration in her classroom.

Mariana Souto-Manning

Mariana is an associate professor at Teachers College, Columbia University. From a critical perspective, she examines the sociocultural and historical foundations of schooling, language development, literacy practices, cultures, and discourses. She studies how children, families, and teachers from diverse backgrounds shape and are shaped by discursive practices, employing a methodology that combines discourse analysis with ethnographic investigation. Mariana is the author of numerous publications, including three books. Mariana is currently the chair of the Early Childhood Assembly of the National Council of Teachers of English.

Kevan Miller

Kevan taught at Bailey's Elementary School in Falls Church, VA, where she was part of a critical literacy study group with Vivian and Carol. She has co-authored and contributed to various publications, including *School Talk* and *Getting Beyond I Like The Book: Creating Spaces for Critical Literacy in K-6 Settings.*

Index